Addiction

To Mum and Dad for having me,
and to Debbie for keeping me.

Addiction

David Marteau

Quay
Books

Mark Allen
Publishing Ltd

Quay Books Division, Mark Allen Publishing Ltd
Jesses Farm, Snow Hill, Dinton, Wiltshire, SP3 5HN

British Library Cataloguing-in-Publication Data
A catalogue record is available for this book

© Mark Allen Publishing Ltd 2001
ISBN 1 85642 189 9

Printed in the UK by The Bath Press, Bath

Contents

Foreword

*And Noah planted a vineyard, and he
drank of the wine and was drunken.*

Genesis 9: 20

It seems that as far back as history has been recorded, mankind has been shortcutting the natural processes of experiencing and feeling reward with mind affecting chemicals. For many, that activity has become a habit, and for many more, it has become a pathological obsession. But despite addiction pervading every major world civilisation throughout history, it has suffered every possible bias and misunderstanding which to some extent continues today. Fortunately, for those of us who want to see through the 'received' prejudices and learn about drug abuse, there are those like David Marteau that have made the subject their life's work and who can impart objectively a wealth of knowledge on this fascinating subject.

This book seeks to treat addiction as a science that we need to understand, and addicts as people that need to be understood. Dr John Marks once compared drug using today to the dangers of ocean sailing in the Middle Ages – but rather than outlaw, demonise or otherwise vilify those who chose to sail, we built lighthouses and drew charts. Let this volume then, be our almanac.

Dr Gordon R Morse
March, 2001

Reference

Marks J (1996) Accidy, addiction and the prohibition. *Addiction Res* **4**(2): i–v

Introduction

This book is small, so omissions have had to be made. It is about the possible causes, nature and treatment of addiction to alcohol and other drugs. It does not concern itself with moderate drink or drug problems; it's about full-on thrown-out-of-Toys-R-Us-at-three-in-the-afternoon addiction. The book discusses compulsive eating and sex, but for reasons of space and ignorance I've left out other addiction-related topics, such as gambling. Please feel free to e-mail me at the following address:

davemarteau@hotmail.com

David Marteau
January, 2001

Part I
Addiction, what it is

1
Addiction: A definition

We can't catch addiction like a common cold. There is no little red bug with a pair of horns sprouting from either side of its head and a big capital 'A' stamped in the gap between them. But in a number of different ways, over generations and generations, people have noticed that some of their family, friends or neighbours appear to have an almost helpless attraction to drink or drugs. They just don't seem able to keep away from the stuff, or they don't appear to know when they've had enough. Words have been put together to describe this destructive pattern: drunkard, low-life, weak-willed, debauched, junkie, alcoholic, bum, over-the-top, hard-core; the list is long. Plainly to the judgement of many of us, something's not right. These habits are at – or beyond – the edge of what civilised twenty-first century citizens allow.

Although experts have debated whether there really is such a thing, many people who live close to someone who makes a habit of 'getting out of their heads' come to believe that they have something wrong with them: a psychological condition. For want of a better word, addiction.

There's no real test for addiction, but there are questionnaires that are pretty reliable at identifying an addiction problem. The best known of these is called CAGE, and it's very short, comprising just four questions:

1. Have you ever felt you should cut down on your drinking?
2. Have people annoyed you by criticising your drinking?
3. Have you ever felt guilty about your drinking?
4. Have you ever had a drink first thing in the morning to steady your nerves or get rid of a hangover (as an eye-opener)?

It's an alcoholism test, but it can be adapted to spot drug addiction by swapping the words 'drug-taking' for drinking.

CAGE is a bit crude. There are more detailed and precise tests, such as the Addiction Severity Index (McLellan *et al*, 1980), and these tend to be used by alcohol and drug researchers when interviewing members of the public, hospital patients, prison in-mates or whoever.

The current standard way of deciding whether or not someone

can be said to be an addict was developed back in the seventies by Griffith Edwards and Milton Gross (Edwards and Gross, 1976). Their ideas can be reasonably broken down as follows (author's comments below each idea):

1. An addict has to use more of a drink or drug to get the same effect.

    OK, but true also of non-addicts who are towards the close of a boozy weekend, or smoking the last joint from a holiday lump of hash.

2. An addict has had the shakes in the morning, or the flu-like symptoms when the heroin's run out.

    This seems reasonable.

3. An addict will drink more alcohol, or take some more drugs, when these withdrawals set in.

    Fair enough.

4. An addict is someone who realises that he or she is compelled to take drink or take drugs.

    This one's thorny and creates more questions than answers. How strong is the compulsion? Does this mean they force themselves to open the bottle or the stash box? Do they have no choice whatsoever?

5. An addict has narrowed down their choice of drugs or drink, and will tend to be rigid about when and where they indulge.

    True, you can set your watch by the habits of some alcoholics and drug addicts, but there are exceptions. Some addicts are all-rounders, taking a whole alphabet of chemicals from alcohol to Valium (or Zodgone, as soon as someone invents it). Other addicts have no real pattern. Binge drinkers, for instance, may stay dry for weeks on end, then go on random benders, drinking anything that's available provided it's not too weak.

6. An addict is someone who devotes large sections of his or her life to seeking-out drink and drugs, to the exclusion of things they really valued in the past.

    This one's spot-on. Once addicted, loved ones, work, 'normal' social activities, and the back lawn are all neglected, while the path to the off-licence or the dealer's is worn to a shine. The addict is ruled less and less by convention and more and more by crack or high-octane cider.

7. If the addict quits, but subsequently goes back to drink or drugs, all of the above starts again.

Usually it does, and very quickly too. It can take a drinker or drug addict years to get messed up over a chemical. If they return to it they can be as bad as they ever were within a matter of days! Gary Smith (2000) believes that there is a point, like a boundary or borderline, that marks the division between addiction and non-addiction. Once someone crosses this line, they become in some way a changed person. From that day on, they are an addict.

Most addiction workers agree that simply being hooked on a drug does not equal addiction. Numerous people in this country have painful medical conditions that are treated with an addictive pain-killer. A number of these patients may develop physical dependence on these drugs (that is to say they become hooked), but after slowly weaning themselves off, the vast majority will not experience a desire to go back on them. They are not true addicts. Many US servicemen returned from the Vietnam War, having used heroin there, presumably to make the experience more bearable. The great majority of them did not go on to develop addiction problems in the years to come, so these people would also probably not have qualified as addicts by most experts' standards (Robins, *et al*, 1974).

My own definition of addiction is, **addiction is a damaging use of drink or drugs despite the best efforts of an individual to reduce or stop**. I'll admit it's not great. Alternatively, it might be said that, **alcoholism and drug addiction are the chemical evasion of self**. This is a bit snappier, but it may be untrue of someone with an addiction problem who has grown up in a house awash with drink and drugs. They might not actually be avoiding themselves – the truth could be that they've been sober or straight so infrequently that they and their true selves have never been properly introduced. I've met many addicts who have said that they really don't know who they are, which is a very distressing state to find yourself in – or to try to find yourself in, to be more correct.

This book often makes a distinction between alcoholics and drug addicts. In fact, a lot of heavy drinkers take other drugs, and enough drug addicts drink heavily. One survey of 72 young people with alcohol problems reported that 96% of these young drinkers took other drugs too (Martin *et al*, 1993). If there are any differences to be found between the two disciplines of being an alcoholic and drug addict, at the risk of making sweeping generalisations I would say that people with alcoholism tend to be older and more conventional. Someone who is addicted to street drugs is on the whole younger, and a bit more rebellious by upbringing or instinct.

Addiction: does it exist?

Noticing the growing discomfort of smokers as a public or works meeting drags on, you'd have to say that addiction probably does exist. Add to this the fact that a good number of smokers want to quit but apparently can't, and the case for addiction looks rock solid. But all we'd be saying here is that some chemicals (eg. nicotine) are so addictive that regular consumption can get us hooked. To then call us 'addicts' would suggest that there's something in us, as well as in the cigarette, that causes the addiction.

So is there something 'wrong' with the addict? Are they, in some way, funny in the head? I don't intend to get too deeply into this question at the moment. I'll put a couple of opposing views and let you decide once you've read as much of this book as will hold your interest.

The 'Anyone can become an alcoholic or drug addict – it's easy' school of thought says that there's no difference in character between an addict and any other member of the public. This is why it takes everyone else so long to twig that 'Mr Normal' is in fact 'Mr Drink-Like-A-Dehydrated-Fish'. It's only several years down the line that 'Mr Fish' becomes unreliable, unpredictable and a bit of a liability. The consistent heavy drinking or drugging have caused his personality to fray at the edges. His bad temper ('What do you mean "Hello?"'), occasional dishonesty ('No I haven't seen your wallet, passport, or valuable collection of rare foreign coins'), and tendency to let you down ('I know, I'm sorry. I forgot it was July'), are all products of his addiction, not causes. He wasn't like that when he started drinking or taking other drugs.

The other point in favour of the argument that addicts don't really exist, is the matter of availability. As I've already suggested, there are no Zodgone addicts in the world, and this is mainly because Zodgone has yet to be invented. Twenty-five years back, there were no crack addicts in Britain. If a society decides to ban alcohol, the number of alcoholics will quickly reduce.

There are approximately ten times more drug addicts in the south west of Scotland than there are in Northern Ireland, just a few miles across the Irish Sea. Intense military security have made it very tricky to smuggle drugs into the Province (Corkery, 1997).

A look at the amount of alcohol different adults drink within a — community reveals that there's no obvious sub-population of alcoholics. The graph does not tail off at three or four drinks per day, only to climb again around ten drinks and over. Instead, there's an even slide from moderate into heavy drinking. Heavy drinking is, in fact, common in the UK: a large mid-90's survey (OPCSa, 1996), revealed that a quarter of all men in this country were drinking above safe limits. Does this mean that one in four of our male compatriots are psychologically disturbed? This seems unlikely.

To finish the point off, it's worth looking at how much we used to drink. Three hundred years ago, when alcohol was cheaper and the personal fitness movement hadn't quite taken off, British people drank more than three times the amount of alcohol we consume today (Spring and Buss, 1977). Were our ancestors three times madder than us? Who was it that built that daft tent in Greenwich?

The addiction-is-a-myth camp has a very strong case. To its followers, the problem is in the bottle, not the drinker. Substances are to blame for addiction. They managed to make their point so strongly that opium was effectively banned in the West, and alcohol was prohibited soon after in all but two of the United States. The most obvious hole in their argument is that if drink and drugs are available to us all, and at roughly the same price, why are all of us not addicted? Or none of us?

After years of working with people who have come to grief on the stuff, I've resisted the temptation to try heroin. If I were to do so, I'm fairly confident that with enough money and perseverance, I could become addicted to it. Would I then be an Addict with a capital 'A'? I don't believe so. But if I went to get a bit of help, (say some free drugs from the friendly NHS, just to tide me over), a nice doctor might then tell me that I may be an addict. Perhaps I should sit down and tell him how it all began. Before too long I might be enjoying all the attention, and thinking about what the expert has told me. 'Yes, I've always felt like a bit of an outsider... It's true that I've drunk beer and smoked cannabis for much of my life... Yes I do get depressed from time to time'. If the doctor is not too hip, I may even exaggerate my drug experiences to make myself appear more daring and extraordinary (Davies and Baker, 1987).

Before meeting 'Dr Feelgood', I had probably picked up all sorts of other labels: laid back, bit of a hippy, nice enough bloke. No-one had ever thought to call me an addict, other than this nice man who gets paid nice money to identify addicts.

John Davies (1997) asks the question; just because someone

keeps doing the same thing, do they need treatment? Do persistent golfers need to be medically monitored? And, come to think of it, should teetotallers be given therapy for their habit of always declining drugs? I suppose the answer is that 50% of murders are not committed by teetotallers, and our hospitals and prisons are not crammed with habitual golfers. Treatment is provided for heavy drinking and drug-taking because society demands it. Something must be done. This is an understandable reaction – to attempt to stop social problems through direct action. But all this 'therapy' still doesn't mean that addiction exists. A teenager can overdose on heroin, alcohol or gas. He or she may have hardly touched a drug in their tragically short life. A young man might rarely drink but he can still be over the limit when on the way home from a party, he runs down a pedestrian. Both of these tragedies involve chemicals, but neither could be fairly seen as resulting from addiction.

However I've met plenty of people who have struggled for years to overcome a compulsion to over-use drink or drugs. They've reached bankruptcy, divorce, and have rattled the cemetery gates. They are as baffled by their problem as everyone around them. It may have taken a while for the penny to drop, and friends and family may not have been thinking in terms of addiction, but they all finally agreed that their loved one has 'a problem' with drink or drugs. That problem can be so large that the person with it takes sanctuary in a hospital or rehab, not through a desire to explore new ways of living, but simply because he or she is in fear of their life.

A sizeable proportion of alcoholics and drug addicts will kill themselves. Different researchers have come up with wildly different results when they've tried to calculate suicide rates. Edwards *et al* (1997) put some of these results together and came up with an average figure for the USA and western countries of 3–4% for alcoholics. This is around 100 times higher than the average for industrialised countries. There are loads of things that can happen in an addict's life (health problems, prison, loss of partner, loss of home, depression), that could make him or her wonder whether it's worth going on. If these negative events are hived off, and counted as other causes for suicide, what's left may be counted as suicide as a response to addiction itself. Harris and Barrowclough (1997) followed a method like this, and came up with the result that people in this country are six times more likely to kill themselves because they're alcoholic, 14 times more likely to do it if they're addicted to opiates (heroin etc.) and 20 times more likely to commit suicide if they're addicted to tranquillisers. Given the strictness of this method, the figures are alarming. Addicts don't always choose overdose as their method of suicide. I've known of people who have hanged themselves rather than carry on fighting their problem. I can recall one dreadful case of a man who stabbed himself to death. His belief in addiction was so complete that he decided to die for it.

Early addiction theories

In a letter to a friend written in 1897, Freud made this point:

> *Masturbation is the one major habit, the 'primary addiction', and it is only as a substitute and replacement for it that the other addictions – to alcohol, morphine, tobacco and the like – come into existence.*

Freud, 1897

So if I've got this right, it's only because we give up masturbating that we become addicted to drugs. Now I don't know about you, dear reader, and I can hardly ask for a show of hands, but I can't honestly believe that everyone comes to the point of abandoning Freud's first addiction prior to picking up chemical problems. What is interesting about Freud's idea (incidentally he was known to be touchy on the question of exactly what his large cigar represented), that pleasure is addictive in itself and that sex and drugs are in some way related, still seems valuable today. Freud's followers (eg. Abraham, 1908) were sometimes obsessed by the idea that men to some degree repress homosexuality, but by drinking loads of beer they can become uninhibited enough to put their arms around a mate, drawl in his ear something about how he really loves him, then pass out on the bathroom floor. These days blokes tend not to be so afraid of hugging each other and being generally a bit less butch, so fear of being gay probably doesn't explain alcoholism very well at all. Certainly it doesn't if you are openly gay anyway, happy to be so, but severely alcoholic as well.

Another theme to the psychologists of a hundred years ago was the effect that very early childhood experiences might have on the finished product – the adult. Freud talked about how, as we grow up, we have to come to realise that we are not the all-powerful beings we felt we were when we were still in nappies. In those days everyone smiled at us, cuddled us, pinched our cheeks, and came running every time we moaned. It must have felt great, like being royalty.

Finding out that we are nothing special after all could be deeply disappointing. But some of us discovered that by getting drunk or stoned, we could feel again that sensation of utter power and satisfaction. We want for nothing. We are in control:

> *Out here on the perimeter there are no stars. Out here we are stoned. Immaculate.*
>
> Jim Morrison, *An American Prayer*, 1970

The one drawback to this magical sense of being effortlessly in control is that it's a complete illusion. Unless mum or dad keep the bottles and the clean clothes and the attention coming, the sense of being 'The Boss' crumbles very fast. A very young child often slips into a state of panic almost as soon as mum leaves the room. She may be gone, and it could be forever for all the little mite knows. When mum returns, the baby is happy again. Mum keeps coming back and gradually we learn that relief and happiness will be ours if we don't panic – there's really no need. We also get to see that Mum has other things to do. It's a depressing thought that mum has a life of her own and that we don't in fact dominate her, but there you go, that's life and we must adjust to its realities.

Addiction theory gets more modern (Tanya)

But what if Mum doesn't always come back, or if when she does she's too upset or preoccupied or exhausted to give us the food and love we need? We can't feel reassured that everything's going to be alright because at various unpredictable times things are a long way from being alright. So, we don't learn that relief and happiness will come back. What we may learn, according to Pine (1990), is that we have to find alternative ways to feel at ease; ways that involve putting our faith in addictive drugs, or intensive relationships which make unreasonable demands on another person.

This is what is at the heart of the emotional theory of addiction; the idea that if we are neglected or mistreated we learn that we can't feel reassured about life, that everything's going to be OK. Things won't be OK unless we get hold of something or somebody to make them that way. Drink and drugs soothe us, and addicts find it almost impossible to stay away from drink or drugs because they have no internal way of calming or soothing themselves (Khantzian, 1981).

The idea that an addict feels generally uneasy and exposed without a drink or a drug may not be the result of a neglectful or cruel upbringing. It might just be that it's a constitutional thing – the unfortunate addict is just made that way. When a problem occurs to which we have no immediate answer, it's common for us to panic. A voice inside our head says that this is a complete disaster and our life is in ruins. Once we've ridden out this horrible wave, a second thought emerges that tells us not to worry; everything is going to be alright. The addict, however, may not possess this secondary reassuring voice. As a miserable result, he or she may spend large periods of a typical week in a state of tension or worry. Alcohol and drugs offer a chemical method to shut out the voice of doom.

There's another way of looking at childhood and the effect that it may have on adult life. A number of people (eg. Kernberg, 1975) believe that a new-born baby (let's say she's a girl and she's called Tanya) doesn't really know she exists. Tanya's aware of colours and shapes and sounds and textures, but she has no language. Without this she can't receive ideas from other older humans. So she won't be familiar with the ideas of identity or life for instance.

Therefore Tanya may not know that she is a person, or that her mum is a person too. She is even less likely to think that she and her mum are separate people. Eventually, as she explores her mother's face with her hands and her eyes, and as she creates responses in her mother by smiling or gurgling, it dawns on Tanya that her mother is a separate being. Or rather, and here Kernberg's idea gets a bit flakey, mum is two separate beings. There's Good Mum who takes care of Tanya and dotes on her, and there's Bad Mum who doesn't attend to Tanya and makes her unhappy. When Good Mum is around everything is great, just perfect. Tanya feels totally satisfied. When Bad Mum turns up, Tanya feels bad too. Very bad.

As the months pass Tanya is able to take the rough with the smooth. She comes to learn that we humans are neither all good nor all bad – we're an irritating mixture of the two. But if Good Mum has been too rarely on the scene, Tanya won't be able to get to this point of regarding mum as a whole person. Too much bad and not enough good makes for an unacceptable deal. Instead (and here Kernberg gets neatly back on track), Tanya will hive off the bad bits: Mum and anyone else who comes to love Tanya will have to be always perfect, ideal; Tanya must not allow herself to feel very bad so she must be perfect too. The alternative is to return to that dreadful feeling of being tiny and without protection. So how does Tanya manage this? By getting into all-or-nothing relationships with people she hopes and believes will be perfect, and by drinking and/or taking drugs to make herself always feel great. She's had too much of feeling terrified and alone and she never wants to go back there again. What's more, Tanya has no idea that all of this is happening. As far as she is concerned she had a very happy childhood. All she knows is that for some reason she keeps getting into relationships that don't last, and that people say she gets out of it too often and she really ought to sort out her drink/drug problem.

All these complex ideas are based on the assumption that addicts can be created – that because someone didn't get the care needed from dad or mum, they eventually turned to chemicals to make themselves feel happy. This may be true for a number of people. Steve Hope *et al's* (1998) study of people born in the UK in 1958, for instance, showed that alcoholism was more common among those who had experienced the divorce of their parents. There is, however, evidence that alcoholism in men is not the result of emotional deprivation (Vaillant, 1983), but a recent British survey concluded that an experience of sexual abuse is unusually common to alcoholics of both sexes (Moncrieff *et al*, 1996).

For women, a neglectful or abusive childhood has been identified as a cause for alcoholism. Interviews with 316 randomly selected Swedish women (Spak *et al*, 1997), indicated that child sexual abuse was an experience the alcoholic women had most in common. In the case of addiction to street drugs, the evidence is strong that an abusive and neglectful past makes women particularly vulnerable to addiction (See *Chapter 2, p. 24*)

This is still a long way from any conclusion that an unhappy past causes addiction. Many people have awful childhoods, but do not go on to become alcoholics or to be dependent on drugs. Likewise, a proportion of alcoholics and drug addicts have not had a nightmare past.

The addict who has suffered a neglectful or cruel childhood learned, probably from an early age, that people are unreliable. You can't trust them. One day the addict-to-be drinks some cider or tries some dope. The effect is dramatic – the addict is taken out of him or herself and transported somewhere else, somewhere far better. When an addict returns to this object of fascination it once again does the job, changing them as dramatically as Alice's potion. At last the addict has found something that will make them feel right. It works every time. It's something you can come to trust, and with trust comes love. A lifelong romance begins.

Craig Nakken puts the matter very neatly:

Addiction is a pathological (sick) *love and trust relationship with an object.*

Nakken, 1996

'Romance' may be going a bit far, but people can become very lyrical around chemicals. A crack addict told me that some guys call the drug the 'beautiful lady in the silver dress'. This beats 'off-white lump of something in tin foil', by some distance. Alcoholics can also become very poetic about the grape and the grain. They've also been known to cuddle their bottle as they doze under the influence of its contents, comforted by the bizarre embrace. And how else can we explain the response of the addict when their loved one says, 'Either the drink goes or I go'? How could he possibly put vodka above his family? In a sense, he must be having an affair with the stuff. Or perhaps he was already spoken for, emotionally married to the bottle before he even met his future wife. Viewed from this angle, it seems horribly inevitable that he should stick with his first true love and look on regretfully as his partner closes the door behind her.

Other addiction theories

The idea that addiction might be some kind of disease has been around for 150 years (Huss, 1851), and it forms the bedrock of Alcoholics Anonymous' approach to addiction. The theory is quite straightforward. It says that alcoholics are suffering from the disease of addiction – they are in some way 'allergic' to alcohol, and if they have a drink they just lose control. This 'disease' is incurable, but it can be stopped from progressing by not drinking at all. Not a drop. The same idea has been transferred to drug addiction – that someone becomes addicted to heroin because they 'suffer' from the disease of addiction.

The disease idea has its critics. 'If it is a disease', they ask, 'how come more people have it when drugs are cheap?' and, 'why is it harder for a poor person to get better than a wealthier one?' It's fair to say that the disease idea almost completely ignores economic or social factors. This makes it very popular with the alcohol industry, for instance, who can produce as much alcohol as possible for the non-diseased. The politicians like it too, as they rake in nice tax revenues while they can't be blamed for the symptoms of 'sick' people. The doctors and nurses don't mind too much either, as it means paid work.

The disease idea is partly right to steer clear of the thought that an unhappy childhood causes addiction. In male alcoholism, the drinking customs that are common to a person's culture are extremely influential. In a major 33-year study, Americans of Irish descent were seven times more likely to develop alcoholism than the sons of Greek, Italian, Jewish, Portuguese or Syrian families (Vaillant, 1983). Another important factor as to whether a person becomes an alcoholic or not is the presence of alcoholism in the family (Drake and Vaillant, 1988). It now appears that drug addiction can be picked up by growing up around heavy drinking and drug-taking. If addiction is an illness, it's one than can somehow be 'learned'.

Estimates vary, but Goodwin's (1992) guess that around one in 25 men and one in a 100 women throughout Europe and America will develop alcoholism at some point in their lives feels about right. In families where one of the parents is alcoholic, the figure climbs to around one in six (Schuckit, 1987). In George Vaillant's (1983) study of over 400 men from one American town, one in three of the sons of alcoholics went on to become alcoholics themselves. This is over eight times the average rate.

The disease idea hinges mainly on the idea of loss of control – that once someone takes a drink or a drug, there's no stopping them. This is examined in *Chapter 16, pp. 131–134*.

A theory that isn't so popular now is the idea that addicts are mad. Knight put the case in 1937:

> *Alcoholism is a symptom rather than a disease… there is always an underlying personality disorder evidenced by obvious maladjustment, neurotic character traits, emotional immaturity or infantilism.*

Knight, 1937

He sounded like a bitter man. Psychiatrists struggled in vain to follow this kind of idea through, searching for the disturbed mind beneath the booze. If they could only get the alcoholic to gain insight, have an understanding of the mental knots that are causing him to drink, he'd be cured. The truth is that insight didn't really work. In some cases it was worse than no treatment at all (Olson *et al*, 1981). Knight's way of viewing alcohol wasn't so different from the disease idea; he just blamed the alcoholic for the sickness. Perhaps his alcoholic patients sensed this, and consoled themselves with a drink.

One of the reasons why a person can become addicted to drink or drugs appears to be a belief that the substance will do certain positive things for them. Making them more relaxed, for example, or helping them to work better, improving the way they come across to other people, and so on.

As a rule, the more good reasons we find for taking a drug, the more likely we are to take it. McCarty *et al* (1983) interviewed almost 600 adults who ranged from teetotallers to alcoholics. He found that the heavy drinkers were far more likely than the light or non-drinkers to believe that alcohol could help them to feel good, forget their worries, and have a good time. They did not share the non-drinkers' view that having several drinks can make them act ridiculously.

If a chemical really does do a useful job (eg. make its consumer feel more relaxed and less bored), stopping is going to be difficult without another activity in place. Even water polo will do. Eventually, drugs being what they are, their relaxing and boredom-busting effects will reduce. If addiction really takes hold, the drugs may even end up going through 180 degrees and actually make the addict feel more tense and bored. The addict may now have fewer positive expectations when he buys the drink or the drug, but it has become a case of 'must have'. Besides, he's no longer in any fit state to play a water-based sport.

2

Addiction: how do people get it?

Poverty and addiction

> *When you ain't got nothing*
> *You've got nothing to lose.*
> Bob Dylan, *Like a Rolling Stone*, 1965

Addiction can flourish when options are limited. There's evidence around that young people who believe that life holds good things in store are less likely to do reckless things – such as take a load of drugs and alcohol – than adolescents who reckon they have little going for them (Jessor *et al*, 1990). A massive study of 160,000 drug-related emergency room admissions across the USA, revealed that black Americans (National Institute on Drug Abuse [NIDA], 1990) were more likely to use hard drugs such as heroin and cocaine than white Americans. Racism and the pressures of poverty would seem to be likely explanations. In the same year as the NIDA study, the American Census Bureau reported that three times more black than white people lived below the poverty line (Pear, 1990). The tendency for poorer people to use stronger or 'harder' drugs is not unique to the USA. A Japanese study (Wada, 1994) calculated that almost three quarters of dope smokers came from high-income families, while only one in 20 amphetamine users had a rich mum or dad.

And a survey of a quarter of a million Americans stated that smoking was 25% more common among people below the poverty line than those on the more comfortable side of it (Flint and Novotny, 1997).

To an extent, where there's urban decay (poor housing, a fragmented community, crime, unemployment, inadequate education), social control has been lost. In these areas social control of drugs has usually been lost too, and public drunkenness, street dealing of drugs, and addiction are rife. Social control is lost; individual control is lost. So it's society's fault? Mmm... it probably wouldn't help someone who's addicted to think in this way, as this means that they are victims of circumstance. Plus, there's always the possibility that educated-enough, privileged-enough, middle-classed people make up some of the residents of these urban twilight zones, having got themselves addicted in the highly ordered suburbs and villages beyond, and drifted nearer the source of their forbidden pleasures.

But to put the responsibility squarely on the shoulder of the addict doesn't make tremendous sense either. If you're poor, you're more likely to stay addicted (Narayan *et al*, 1996). If we allow certain drugs to be broadly available, ie. alcohol and nicotine, we probably don't have the right to feel completely innocent when we learn that these two are far and away the biggest chemical killers in our society, doing their worst damage to the already disadvantaged. Together they kill about 160,000 UK citizens per year (Home Office, 1998; OPCS, 1996b). It's not good. Illicit or 'street' drugs kill fewer than 3,000 of us each year, but as drug addicts often drink and smoke pretty liberally, more drug deaths are likely to be hidden in with the 'legal' 160,000. It's a massive number, and the problem is not confined to Britain. In Finland, for example, too much drinking is the cause of 40% of all male deaths under the age of 50 (Makela, 1998). In America, drunk driving is the main cause of death for men under 25 (Little and Clontz, 1994).

As John Marks has pointed out (1996), addiction is influenced by price and availability. There are more alcoholics in Britain than Saudi Arabia, and it's relatively safe to say that this is in part down to the lack of available alcohol in Saudi. In Svalbard, a region of Norway, the drink is cheaper than anywhere else in the country and consumption is 50% higher (Høyer *et al*, 1994). Cheapness and legality can't be the whole story, otherwise as a nation we'd all be hopelessly addicted to glue or methylated spirits. There are some people who will spend plenty and risk even more, just to get hold of some Johnnie Walker in Riyadh, or heroin in Birmingham. There's also a question of fashion, with drugs coming in and out of favour at various points over the past century. Cocaine, for instance, was tremendously popular in America at the start of the 1980s. By the end of the decade prices had remained stable but consumption had fallen by a half (NIDA, 1989). People apparently got bored with the stuff, although no doubt some of them found other chemical interests to fill the gap. Addiction is therefore, the product of price, availability and demand: where the demand comes from, and what can be done about it, are the themes of this book.

Culture

A survey (Glassner and Berg, 1980) of a substantial number of Jews living in New York did not identify a single alcoholic. There may be no single reason why this community appeared immune to alcoholism, but Jewish culture generally discourages heavy drinking. A similar absence of drinking problems might be found among Jews in London or Belgrade. As a rule, drunkenness is not acceptable within Jewish societies, and heavy drinking is associated with other cultures and peoples. Perhaps, by way of compensation, food holds prized status within the Jewish world. The Friday Shabbat Dinner is an important global ritual, and individual festivals demand special and particular dishes. Chicken soup is traditionally regarded as 'God's penicillin', a non-alcoholic counterpart to the gentile 'medicinal brandy'. Where Anglo-Saxons will 'wet the baby's head' (ie. find another sound reason to drink too much), a Jewish family may celebrate the birth of a male child at a Bris, a cultural event where food is central. The gentile head-wetters, by contrast, may fetch the girls a bag of crisps back from the pub. Alcoholism is therefore rare, but obesity can be a scourge for older Jewish people (McQueen, 2000).

It's not good that approximately 3% of the total adult Western population seem to have chosen to poison themselves. Aren't there any less dangerous ways of relaxing the mind? We've all got televisions after all.

Alcohol has been a part of our culture for thousands of years. A particularly early account of alcohol abuse can be found in the Bible, where Noah is said to have drunk too much wine and been discovered crashed out in his tent (Genesis 9, 20–23). To be fair, he saved the entire planet, so he must be classified as a good bloke. The New Testament also gave alcohol a reasonable press with Jesus turning water into wine at the wedding feast of Canna. According to the Gospels, Christ invested wine with even more significance by performing the ritual of the Last Supper, describing wine as his blood. It's impossible to say how much of an effect these stories have had on the way Western culture now looks upon drinking, but had Judas 'sold' Jesus for alcohol rather than gold, it's conceivable that drink would now be seen in a poorer light. And the goings-on in the Garden of Eden probably didn't do snakes any favours.

So, is it possible that a change in culture can influence addiction? The answer is probably yes, and two examples come to mind.

The first occurred in North America with the coming of conquering Europeans. Prior to their arrival, many native American tribes in what is now southwestern USA produced their own alcoholic drinks, often from fermented cactus (Waddell and Everett, 1980). It would seem that drunkenness was not a big problem among these peoples until their introduction to heavy whisky drinking by the white frontier settlers. Exposure to this kind of drinking, coupled with a permanent loss of tribal ways and liberties, resulted in levels of problem drinking far in excess of anything known before. To some extent, Native American culture has not yet recovered from these Wild West events.

The second example is an instance of how cultural change can reduce addiction. In China at the time of the 1949 Revolution, opium had been a massive social problem which severe punishment, even execution, could not solve. What the new political system brought to China was a sense of purpose and change, two qualities which are the opposites of the addiction norms of aimlessness and repetition. On top of this came land reforms which took the ground away from opium growers. Education and employment improved, and a new sense of social responsibility was encouraged. This was all exciting stuff, and much of it made drug addicts seem embarrassingly out of step. The spirit of hope that is common when something big and new is unfolding also pushed drug abuse on to the back foot, as addiction prefers the fertile soil of hopelessness and defeat, as we've seen among Native Americans and Aboriginal Australians. Chinese communism eventually brought its own unique kinds of misery to the people, and there's plenty to be said about the disadvantages of a single-party state and rule by propaganda and fear. Nonetheless, the huge changes in China since 1949 have shown that addiction can be substantially reduced by political and cultural change (Lowinger, 1977).

Today we are approaching a time when the use of street drugs is permitted within British youth culture. The last couple of dubious drugs are the twin demons of smack and crack, and even they are beginning to gain some acceptability. Much of the impetus to resist drugs came from the youth of China who were singled out for a programme of empowerment and indoctrination by Mao Tse Tung during the Cultural Revolution of the 1960s. By contrast, we were offered the fat lad from Grange Hill singing, 'Just say "No"'.

Well-intentioned and deeply musical in its own way, but hardly as radical and far-reaching as the Chinese response to the international drug menace.

The truth may be that as a nation we don't want to say no. We are not prepared to do what is really necessary to defeat addiction by acting as each other's moral policemen, demanding zero tolerance and notifying the authorities on the slightest suspicion of our neighbours' involvement in anything from dope to heroin. It's a bit too George Orwell for our tastes. Live and let live, that's what we say. It's their business – they know the risks. I'm not getting involved. In fact more and more of us **are** getting involved, smoking a bit of dope, taking the odd 'E', maybe even a line of coke at a party. These are the days when self-denial seems pointless.

British culture also makes considerable allowance for heavy drinking. There are numerous things we say that describe the act of drinking, expressions that seem to carry the message that it's alright really to get drunk. Examples could include:

I'd had a good drink – not, interestingly, a bad drink

I got completely legless – the implication here appears to be that drinking to the point of collapse is something we needn't be ashamed of; it's funny and fairly clever.

I was out of my head – Again, it's a laugh, drinking to the point of oblivion.

Of course, I'd had a few – What could be more natural?

Rat-arsed, pissed, paralytic, we've got a rich fund of ways to describe drunkenness. The British don't generally speak of themselves as being disgracefully drunk. Our culture, in the expression of its language, permits most of us to drink heavily.

The Chinese don't have the same magnitude of alcohol problems as the West, either. Li and Rosenblood's 1994 survey found that Chinese Canadians drank 'significantly less' than white Canadians. Oriental Flush (see *Chapter 5, p.45)* explains this in part, but traditional Chinese disapproval of drunkenness may be an important factor.

The West generally must hold its hands up. Television, the music business and the movies have all glamourised drink and drugs. Hazan *et al* (1994) watched 62 of the top movies from 1960–1990, and found that in terms of their time 'on screen' the characters smoked three times more cigarettes than the average American. Smoking among young actors more than doubled. Tobacco companies, on the basis of a 'product placement' deal, fund many Hollywood movies.

Cultural influences can be local rather than ethnic or national. de la Fluente *et al* (1997) found that the proportion of heroin addicts injecting their drug as opposed to smoking it varied widely between three Spanish cities. In one city injecting was three times more popular than in another. Britain is a patchwork of drug types and habits, with crack ruling the roost in some southern and north-western towns, and heroin predominating in other areas. There are further local outbreaks of tranquilliser or amphetamine addiction, like rashes of satellite dishes on a residential estate.

Emotion

Addicts and alcoholics have often said that they have gone back to addiction as a result of difficult emotions (Marlatt and Gordon, 1985). For some reason, people with addiction problems tend to find it hard to take the knocks that life can dish out. Their worldly or brash exteriors can conceal a hive of worries and doubts. Or are they just deceiving us? Don't they just drink because it's very nice, or use heroin because it's less hassle than many other lifestyle options, such as getting a job? And what about that 'My Cocaine Nightmare' tabloid stuff? Must have been hell.

We know it's true that there are definite advantages to drinking or stoning the day away, particularly if it happens to be a Monday. The sunlight splitting the smokey pub air, languid armchair afternoons spent watching the world struggle by. And we're supposed to feel sympathetic? I would be willing to say that there's enough evidence out there to show that people take drugs in part to get through the tough times. Of course, drinking and taking drugs to excess can makes life tough but, that aside, the everyday ebb and flow of emotions we almost all experience seem to be very tricky for a proportion of addictive persons to take. By hypnotically inducing bad moods such as depression and anger in their volunteers, Childress *et al* (1992) found that they could trigger cravings in 'clean' opiate users. The smoker will smoke more heavily than usual when the pressure's on. The drinker will tell his mate that he, 'could murder a pint', after a bad day.

Alcohol and street drugs, taken in the right quantities, can alter our mood. They each have their own way of doing this, and the new moods they offer appeal to some of us but not to others. Some people love the unrestricted carefree feeling that alcohol creates in them, while others hate the out-of-control confusion of drunkenness. For them the honed sharpness of speed is the way to go, while the hippy next door dislikes having his nerves jangled to that extent. He recommends heroin, for that feel-easy-anywhere feeling. We choose our poisons.

It's often been said that the addict is unknowingly taking a kind of medicine. The natural way to live is in balance, and we look for this harmony on every level of life. If we're tired we rest, if we're cold we put on another layer of clothing, if we're agitated we try to relax. This is true to an extent when it comes to drinking and drug-taking, but it doesn't tell the whole story. The amphetamine addict, for instance, is often a naturally speedy person, always on the move; entertaining, but tiring to be around. If there's one thing he doesn't need, it's something to quicken him up. We probably all know someone who is warm and friendly, great to be around. Yet when they get a drink inside them, they can turn argumentative and obnoxious (Fishbein *et al*, 1993). Plain nasty. Again, they're drawn to the one chemical they should avoid at all costs.

What may be going on here is that the addict is trying to put some distance between himself and how he or she feels. Deep down the speedy addict may have all sorts of finer and more complex moods, but he has the energy to out-pace these. A bit more fuel in the tank and it's Goodnight Vienna. The warm and friendly alcoholic may already be emotionally half out the door. Be honest, for what proportion of the day would you say that you feel warm and friendly? The amiable alcoholic has learned to smile though his heart is aching, and a warm and friendly drug like alcohol can keep the avoidance of truer emotions at bay.

I suppose I've argued against myself here, and that the alcoholic and addict are in a way looking for balance by topping up their imbalanced way of dealing with the world. They're searching for a magical answer to the emotional demands of life by engaging in a sort of internal alchemy.

Narcotics Anonymous (1988) make the observation that:

> *Before coming into the Fellowship, we either felt elated or depressed.*

This emotional 'either/or' is a common experience in people who are stuck in addiction. A range of more subtle emotions in between these extremes, such as concern, contemplation or unease are not so easily recognised and accommodated. Addicts often bunch these moods together under the general heading of boredom, and then head for the pub.

Addiction isn't necessary an avoidance of life. Many addicts are vital people who, if anything, have too much appetite for life. Drugs can heighten experience as well as block it, and this life at a heightened level, or 'high life', can be very addictive. After all, who wants mediocrity?

In the end the addict's life plan goes into free fall, but the addict can't pull out as he has no other method of living. He's guilty but he can't handle that, he's panicky and he can't handle that either. All he knows is the thing that used to work but just won't any more – the drug. But he sticks with it, as he can't cope without it. But he's angry much of the time as his life is going from diabolical to worse still. His anger keeps most of the people who care for him at bay. Many disappear altogether, making him resentful. His former employer, first wife, elder son and even his ageing mum and dad are endlessly criticised and blamed. He sees other people getting on with their lives and he becomes sick with jealousy as his accelerates in reverse. He makes desperate attempts to keep someone with him, a protector. He emotionally blackmails them, saying that he doesn't know what he'd be forced to do if they leave. Held emotional hostage, they don't leave. He treats them appallingly as his self-contempt grows. They do leave. He plagues them with out-of-his-head visits at three in the morning. He's the drowning man who, in his panic, pulls his would-be rescuer under with him. He tries to kill himself. Fancy a pint?

Gender

She learned, to her dismay, that she only felt loved when she wasn't herself .

Joel Covitz, 1986

I can tell that you can't be who you pretend.

Syd Barrett, *No Good Trying*, 1970

Women are less likely than men to use almost any drug. An exception is prescribed drugs such as tranquillisers and anti-depressants. In the USA 69% of all of these prescriptions are for women (Winick, 1992). This may be because women are more open to talking about their feelings. They are often prepared to take their emotional problems to a doctor, who may then give them mood-altering medicines. Men, by contrast, tend to keep their feelings well-hidden and take them to the barman, who will then give them some mood-altering beer.

Traumatic events in a woman's childhood and adult life seem to make her more susceptible to addiction than a man who had suffered a troubled life. Miller *et al* (1987) found that 67% of alcoholic women she interviewed had reported being sexually abused by an adult during childhood. To provide a comparison, she also spoke with a group of non-alcoholic women of similar age and background. Only 28% of these women stated that they had been abused in childhood.

Childhood sexual abuse is not rare within a home where one or both parents are drinking or using drugs heavily. It's often not the father who is the abuser, but an outside male who has been allowed access to the child through the neglect of the parents. Hagan (1987) interviewed a group of drug addicts from the United States. Eighty-three per cent of them reported that they had been brought up in a home where chemicals were abused. Two-thirds of the women stated that they had been sexually assaulted, and 60% said that they'd been beaten.

Perhaps most upsetting of all, almost all of the interviewees said that they had grown up wishing they were someone else. It would appear that they found a chemical method to change themselves into that someone else. In our culture the traditional female role is one of maternal self-denial. Were a woman to move so far from this into the apparent reckless self-indulgence of addiction, she invites not only the condemnation of the rest of us, but also herself. She may well feel that she has 'failed' to become a worthwhile woman. For her to go beyond the bounds of what she behoves to be acceptable, it would follow that something has been pushing her in this direction. Her life prior to addiction must have been hard to tolerate. Although this is a generalisation, it's true of many women.

There's certainly evidence that women with addiction problems have higher levels of anxiety, depression and lower self-worth than the average non-addicted woman (Blume, 1992; Wang *et al*, 1998). This is probably not just down to the shameful quality of addiction: Schutte *et al* (1997) found that young females who already had signs of depression had an above-average risk of going on to develop drinking problems.

Bulimia is more common in addicted women (Ross et al, 1988), and this can persist as a problem long after the drug addiction has been arrested. Women are also more likely to develop drug problems if they already drink heavily (Schmitz et al, 1993).

Women are 51% water, men are 65% (Van Thiel et al, 1988). As most drugs (including alcohol) are water-soluble, a standard dose of a drug is more concentrated and therefore greater in its effect upon women. Lower average body weight makes the drug stronger still. Women also absorb alcohol more thoroughly (Frezza et al, 1990) and more quickly than most men (Cole-Harding and Wilson, 1987). The result is that women are prone to a more rapid development of addiction than men (Corrigan, 1980). This vulnerability to the effect of drugs also means that women's health can be damaged earlier in addiction than the health of men (Gavaler, 1982). An alcoholic woman can expect to die 15 years earlier than a non-alcoholic female of her own age, and sooner than an alcoholic man (Lindberg and Agren, 1988). Female drug addicts can die more easily than male addicts (O'Doherty and Farrington, 1997).

In view of the stigma it attracts, women do not tend to drink as openly as men (Glatt, 1982). Social disgrace is probably also the prinicipal reason why the family of an alcoholic woman is less likely to admit she has a problem than that of an alcoholic male (Beckman, 1975). Even relatively heavy-drinking cultures can be intolerant of female drinking. Harrison et al (1993), for instance, found that women in Ireland were less likely to drink than females from England and Wales.

As mentioned elsewhere (Chapter 11, p.95) an alcoholic or addict partner can have a considerably bad influence on the ability of a woman to resist addiction (Goehl et al, 1993; Heath et al, 1989). Female heroin addicts are less likely to inject than men, but they are more likely to be living with a partner who takes drugs, which makes quitting a bit of a headache, as it's incredibly difficult to stay off when the stuff is right under your nose.

Smoking is a real peril for women these days, with a rapid increase in young female smokers both in Europe and the USA (Escobedo and Peddicord, 1997). No-one has got to the bottom of this dangerous trend. Nichter et al (1997) reported that teenage girls had told them that they smoked to reduce stress. However, Thomsson (1997) reported that females smoke more when they're happy and relaxed. Byrne et al (1993) couldn't find any psychological reasons why young Australian women were taking up smoking. They felt that it was a lot to do with the smoking habits of family and friends.

Probably true. Weight control is another possible reason why more adolescent girls are smoking.

Weight control and body image are persistent themes to female addiction problems. Cochrane *et al* (1998) found that almost half of the women addicts they interviewed took coke and drank alcohol as a way to lose weight. This diet plan has yet to be endorsed by *Woman's Own* magazine.

3
Addictive thinking

Doctors and nurses have been given the job of 'treating' alcoholics and drug addicts because our nation has come to the conclusion that people with addictive problems are ill. Plainly, someone who has abused their body to the point where they have an inflamed liver or a serious lung infection is unwell, and with time and a few tablets they can be as fit as the next person. Yet they then go right back to the source of their sickness, despite all the costs and warnings. They must be mad! But an addict is as sane as the next person. Addicts are capable of making sense of the world in every respect except when it comes to seeing that their heavyweight consumption of drink or drugs may just explain why things in their life tend to go so regularly and badly wrong.

I suppose this, then, is a kind of mini-madness, confined to one area of what a person does, as if they were in the habit of walking barefoot on broken glass and forever wondering why their feet hurt. A similar thing has been said of anorexia, that it represents a kind of insanity where the sufferer is in every other way completely rational, but upon seeing her or his reflection in a mirror, they become deluded. They 'see' that they are fat and should therefore eat less. Everyone else, meanwhile, sees that they're far too thin and a good dinner wouldn't do them any harm. Here the comparison begins to break down a little: everyone else around an alcoholic thinks that they should drink less; the alcoholic secretly might agree. It's unlikely that he believes he drinks too little. A heavy drinker will sometimes say, 'I know I drink a bit too much'. They realise that it's going on, and it may be pride rather than craziness that blocks them from being more honest about the problem and saying, 'I know I drink considerably too much'. No-one likes to admit that they're out of order, and getting drunk and misbehaving can put someone squarely in 'the wrong', not just in the judgement of others, but in their own eyes as well. To be frequently acting in a way which we ourselves regard as incorrect, causes the appearance of those twin giants of negative emotion – guilt and shame. These mortifying feelings are hard to shake off, but more drink and drugs represent a quick method of escape.

There's a second and more obvious factor that makes it difficult to own up to an addiction problem, and that is the fear of giving up. A considerable avenue of pleasure would be permanently closed off, friendships may have to end, and life will have to be faced without the comfort of a chemical refuge. Rather than take all of this on, it makes far more sense to say, 'I've got it under control now', and drift off down the pub as soon as the domestic coast is clear.

The difficulty addicts encounter in 'seeing' that they have a problem is also related to the company they keep. In Britain, male heavy drinkers tend to congregate in pubs. In this environment your level of alcohol consumption is normal. Your glass is no bigger than anyone else's, and there's always someone who drinks more than you each night.

I was drinking in a pub one day with a couple of blokes and they started talking about one of the regulars, Terry, who had recently 'gone off the rails' and been taken into the local psychiatric unit. Sounded like he'd had some kind of alcohol-fuelled breakdown. 'Do you suppose he could be an alcoholic?' one of the guys asked. By his tone it was clear that this was a long shot, a possibility about as remote as Terry being a closet astronaut. In the end all agreed that the extraordinary might be true – Terry could be an alcoholic. But his two mates did not see any connection between Terry's current difficulties and their own habits. The fact that they were his regular drinking partners had no bearing on their use of alcohol whatsoever. Come to think of it, what was I doing there? No need to be silly about this; what could be more normal and natural than having a pint after a hard day's work? I suppose the word 'denial' has no relevance here.

I chatted to a male alcoholic who told me about how he'd lost a well-paid job because of his drinking. He wasn't too bothered; he still had plenty of money in the bank, so he decided to take it easy for a while. He met a few guys around town who liked a drink, and because he was flush and they weren't, he'd buy them a few beers and they'd chat and hang out together. The day came when the money finally ran out, he couldn't pay the rent and he was evicted from his flat. He met up with his mates in the park and told them about his problem. 'Don't worry', said one of the men, 'You can always stay here', 'Where?' says my client, not getting it at all. 'Here, in the park. We do'. It then dawned on him that they were tramps, and now, to all intents and purposes, so was he. Up until that moment he'd honestly believed he was a businessman taking a well-earned rest.

Addicts seem to have a particular blind-spot when it comes to the dangers of drink and drug use. Catherine McGregor (1998) interviewed a group of Australian heroin addicts about the riskiness of their hobby. Almost three quarters of them told her that they 'rarely' or 'never' worried about taking an overdose. They were probably far more concerned with where the next heroin was coming from. After getting that they may 'rarely' or 'never' worry about anything much for a few hours. Alcoholics are good at not perceiving danger too, claiming that alcohol is actually good for you, or that they drive better when they've had a drink. McCarty *et al* (1983) asked heavy drinkers if they felt that they might injure themselves as a result of taking six or more drinks. They thought this was highly unlikely. In fact, alcoholics are four times more likely than a sober citizen to injure themselves in the home or walking down the street (Hillbom and Holm, 1986).

In a strange way drug addicts also see themselves as doing the normal and natural thing. Thanks to the growth in international travel and to current public taste, drugs are common enough, but drug users may tell you that, 'drugs are everywhere' or, (pointing to the latest sniff-and-tell celebrity scandal), 'everyone's at it'. It's true, of course, of the drug sub-culture, as in this group drugs are what you do. To an addict, the non-drug culture is a mysterious and distant land inhabited only by born-again Christians, formation ballroom dancers and anyone over 85. You'd no sooner want to go there than Siberia in February.

So drugs are the sensible option. Putting a needle into your arm is not, however, so sensible, and all but the smallest percentage of drug takers do not begin taking drugs in the hope that some day they'll be lucky enough to inject themselves. Most drug addicts will tell you that that was one thing they swore they'd never do. Smoking a drug is normal. Even sniffing one. But pulling brown stuff up into a syringe and stabbing it into your veins is totally different. Yet ask a drug addict why they changed their mind, and their answer is probably about the stuff working out too expensive, or that smoking or sniffing wasn't having a strong enough effect any more, or somebody offered to show them how one night and... In my experience the answer is very rarely, 'because by then I was seriously addicted to drugs'. By that time the heavy drug user may, without fully realising it, have drifted into a world where injecting drugs is as normal as mowing the grass on a Sunday. As a rule, drug addicts do not have well-maintained lawns.

But there are other explanations for people injecting themselves with drugs. Although it's dangerous, the sensation that injecting can produce as the drug rushes straight into the brain of the user is so exciting that little else can compare with it. Skydiving, white-water rafting and bungee jumping are all candidates, but none of these are exactly safe either. So the drug injector engages in some form of armchair extreme sport. A client told me a few weeks ago that there's a growing trend among Londoners in their mid-teens for going straight to injecting heroin, rather than poncing about with the preliminary stages of sniffing or smoking the stuff. It's all for the sake of the thrill, and it sounds very worrying.

Injecting can be dictated by economic need. In America, during the Prohibition years, there were reports of alcoholics injecting themselves with methylated spirits (Marks, 1997). This obviously doesn't happen now. Maybe an injecting drug addict is poor rather than 'sick'. But there still seems to be something unnatural and not right about injecting yourself. Neumark and Anthony (1997) believe that they've found evidence that people who show behavioural problems in childhood are more likely to become injectors. There was no apparent connection between early troubled behaviour and non-injecting drug use.

We don't generally regard what we do as abnormal or sick. Someone with an addiction problem is no different in viewing him or herself as an average kind of person who likes a drink now and then, or a bit of coke. But of course they are different in that their consumption is of a different magnitude to the 'normal' citizen. They have what Jim Orford (2000) calls an excessive appetite. It comes down in part to exactly how much is 'a bit' of coke, how many drinks constitute 'a drink'. People with excessive appetites are often the last to recognise this fact. They are puzzled by the modest intake of those around them. They tend to shake their heads and mutter something vaguely disparagingly about 'lightweights'. A male alcoholic I had been working with told me that he had been trying to quit the booze, so he'd gone to an Alcoholics Anonymous meeting. He struck up a friendship there with another bloke, but his new friend didn't turn up for a few weeks. When he eventually did show, he arrived looking pretty rough. 'Where have you been?' asked my client. 'Oh I've been bad', his mate said, 'Totally out of control, drinking 15 pints of Guinness a night'. My client told me the only thought that entered his head upon hearing this news was, '15? Why only 15?' He was appalled by the man's lack of application.

There's another strand to addictive thinking, which is the belief or presumption that some addicts have that life should be sweet all of the time. I don't know where they get this daft idea from, Walt Disney perhaps, but it can make an addict's life a tantalising agony.

The poor addict struggles under the misapprehension that life isn't 100% lovely because something is not quite right. The rest of us have come to the more depressing conclusion that everything isn't 100% lovely because most things aren't quite right, and we might as well get on with it all the same. By contrast, the addict is looking for perfection, and this quest makes demands on him or herself as well as all those around. Things must be done to the highest possible standard – cleaning, cooking, working.

This may not tie up with some people's experience of the couch potato addict, or the drinker who lives in a pigsty of empty bottles and full ashtrays, but the theory goes that these people are perfectionists too. As they can't find the perfect job, or live in the perfect house, or sustain the perfect relationship, they might as well not even bother trying. If you scratch the surface with an addict who is destined never to make the feature pages of *Ideal Home* magazine, you may find someone with a highly idealised and perfectionist opinion of how life should be. This is the kind of defiant spirit that can make an addict appear such a doomed romantic to the more stolid and sober citizen.

Addictive thinking has been described by Alcoholics Anonymous as 'stinking thinking'. They plainly don't value it. Examples of thought patterns that can feed addiction are not hard to find. There's the catastrophic reaction for instance, which goes along the lines of, 'Oh no, the alarm clock battery's flat, and there's no way I can get one at this hour, and I'm bound to oversleep and lose that job. Sod it, what drugs have we got around at the moment?' The catastrophist doesn't so much admit defeat as welcome it.

Self-pity is also another thought pattern common to addiction. This runs something like, 'I loved that job. Why did that clock have to stop last night? Nothing goes right for me. What drugs have we got around at the moment?'

Thought patterns are habitual. They become established because they serve a purpose. Someone who is taking an exam will be plagued by thoughts about the need to study. When a baby is born, the little one's needs will dominate his or her parent's thinking. I am currently sick of thinking about this book. Once the exam is sat, the baby grown up and this book finished, the pattern of thinking is broken, but not before. For as long as addiction is in residence, the patterns of thinking that feed it will persist.

So why does addiction need its own pattern of thinking? Won't a single thought like, 'lager' do? For some it may, but we're not beasts, and we've been trained and taught to be ashamed when we act like them. We're not even allowed a good scratch in public, so to drink ourselves stupid, or burn the day away in a stoned haze, is not commendable. What we really need is an excuse, so that we can justify addiction to ourselves as much other people. Back to the patterns.

Black-and-white thinking is one that helps addiction: 'You're either for me or against me'. If they're for us, then they agree that the way we live our life is acceptable. If they're against us, they're a vindictive little toe-rag who has set out to make trouble. 'I can't believe the way she treated me. That's done me, that has. What drugs have we got around at the moment?'

Selective hearing borders on addictive thinking. The tactic here is to engage in a conversation with someone and when they say something that allows your addiction to continue, latch on to that and disregard everything else. 'You said, "I don't give a toss what you do". No, no, that's what you said. So you can't suddenly turn round and tell me I can't do this or that. You don't give a toss, remember? Right, what drugs have we got around at the moment?'

Mills *et al* (1993) interviewed 100 students. They found that the more alcohol someone regularly drank, the less likely they were to regard excessive drinking as a problem. It would appear that denial sets in early.

Addictive thinking doesn't mean an addict or alcoholic has got a brain that can't think straight. On the contrary, he or she has a brain that thinks straight to its target: chemicals. This means a massive mental overhaul, as Narcotics Anonymous poetically point out:

Our best thinking got us into trouble.

NA, 1988

They go on to put the case even more bluntly:

What we knew about living... almost killed us.

NA, 1988

Brain reward

The single fact that underlies most drug-taking is that it feels good. Unless they're drastically disturbed, people don't rub chilli powder into both eyes on a daily basis. It hurts. Pleasure, on the other hand, is something we all tend to repeat.

In 1957, Killam *et al* came up with evidence that certain drugs work on areas of the brain that are specifically geared-up for the manufacture of that unbeatable sensation, pleasure. These certain drugs are addictive.

In a nutshell, what we all possess is a circuit in the core of our brains that rewards us when we do something that helps the human species to survive. What we experience as a swell of pride when we redecorate the home, or when our kids do well at school, or we get a top job, is the pleasure that comes from providing a secure future. Our brain rewards us. So pleasure has a purpose. The problem for humans is that we're smart enough to by-pass the hard bit and get straight to the prize. Alcohol, heroin, cocaine, you name it, they each find a way to activate our pleasure switches. They do it by differing routes, some by making us over-produce certain pleasure chemicals in the brain, others by instructing our brains to trap and save up ridiculously high amounts of these very nice chemicals as they drift through. They deceive the brain into thinking that important survival needs are being met and everything's going sweetly. In fact, vital needs are not being met, things are going badly sour, and the addict is headed towards death, not life.

This reward system of the brain is centred on a busy junction of nerve cells in the middle or core of our brains. It's called the nucleus acumbens and its location is at one end of a mesh of brain cells which terminates in some very welcome 'reward cells' towards the front of the brain. Along this corridor of cells we have nerves that house (or garage, you could say) a brain chemical called dopamine. Dopamine is a complicated chemical which performs a number of different tasks in the mind, but the one that concerns us here is the transmission of reward, making us feel good all over. Dopamine does this by latching on to neighbouring cells and passing the message of pleasure on, like some lightning fast children's party game. We can be fairly sure that dopamine is at the heart of drug-taking, as people who have been given tablets which stop dopamine from latching on to their brain cells have temporarily lost interest in food and even water (Wise, 1989).

Some human activities that trigger the brain reward circuits are virtually all fun and little work. Top of the list is sex, since it's vital that we reproduce or there will be no-one left to sell something to in the future. Not far behind (and ahead in some of us) comes food. If we were to suddenly become not particularly interested in food we'd be at risk of fading away as a species. Because they share the capacity to give us loads of pleasure for not much effort, both sex and food are regarded by a number of people as addictive. In a way they can both ruin your life if they get a hold of you. The persistent over-eater risks heart disease and rejection by society for being too fat. The person who is compelled to get as much sex as possible may wreck a happy family life or contract a serious disease by playing the field too freely.

If these are addictions then they can't be true chemical addictions since they don't involve the taking of a mind-altering drug. Yet, as I've tried to explain, drugs don't directly get you high. Instead, they tap into and adjust our own in-built high system. For instance, a computer expert was recently fixing my machine at work. Peter told me that he had taken six months to crack a software bug on another customer's system. The problem was complicated, and at times he thought that he'd never solve it. One evening he clicked the mouse and the whole knot unravelled on the screen right in front of him. He was so happy that he began to cry: 'The feeling I got was much higher than any of these people here can get with their heroin or what-have-you', he told me. But for their first ecstasy pill, first pipe of crack or first hit of heroin, he was right, as his brain had been showered with a rewarding chemical.

The feeling Peter had had that evening was the same as these initial drug experiments as they represent two separate doors to the same room. Peter is not now chasing another six-month brain-twisting riddle to re-experience that golden ecstatic moment but, all around the globe, drug users are chasing their own chemical passport to repeat that wonderful feeling. Their problem is that the experience is never as powerful the second, third, or five hundredth time. Crack addicts, for instance, frequently say of their habit, 'You're always trying to chase that feeling you got the first time, but you can never get there'. In fact, they tend to fall further and further short of the target. Because they can get close enough to make it pleasurable, and because six months of intensive work isn't involved each time around, some people just keep pressing the button. The addict has worked out a system for having his puddings without ever eating his greens.

In fact, with the help of a surgeon and an electrician, pressing a button is all you have to do, as a researcher called Heath (1964) found out when he arranged for people to have their pleasure centres wired up and turned on. It worked just as well as any drug known to man.

So what does all this tell us? Three things really: that alcohol and drug users have found a way of hacking into their personal happiness systems; that the pleasure that drink and drugs trigger in the brain draws some of us back and back again for more; and that all the effects that drink and drugs provoke in us are as natural as joy or love. This last point is interesting as people with addictive problems often experience an infatuation with their favoured chemical. Alcoholics may collect fine wines or rare beers, they might even get their own pub and surround themselves with a moat of booze. A drug addict may spend hours every day in an unswerving pursuit of heroin or crack, risking almost anything to get hold of the object of their desire. Under its influence they may repeatedly study the stuff, turning it over in their hands. In conversation they'll persistently speak its name like an act of religious devotion or romantic love.

In a way it's scientifically correct to say that the alcoholic or the addict is captivated by his or her own brain, rather than by vodka or crack cocaine. The obsession is therefore in truth with the self. This is one reason why alcoholics and addicts are sometimes regarded as self-centred. They're not really, but they could at times be described as self-absorbed. This makes quitting a very tough prospect, as the brain – the one thing that is going to get the addict out of the trap of addiction – is the critical component of the trap itself. We'll return to this dilemma later.

What about brain punishment – the rolling pin over the head as 'alckie' dad creeps in after midnight, or the severe loss of money that comes from a big addiction? When the negatives outweigh the positives, perhaps the brain reward system will be overpowered by areas of the nervous system that transmit misery and woe. In other words, if it's all in the name of pleasure, why doesn't addiction stop at the point where the fun ends? There are three possible answers to this. Number one is that the brain reward idea is wrong. It's only a theory, and there may be a better explanation for addiction just waiting to be discovered. It's a fairly sound theory, but it doesn't seem to answer the observation of Joseph *et al* (1996) that bad experiences as well as good ones can increase the amount of dopamine in our brains. My own brain can't cope with this one, so I'll let you try to figure it out, and move on to answer number two, which is that the addiction can't stop as by this point the addict is already in too deep – they're hooked, and what's more, they've forgotten how to gain pleasure from any other activity ('Go to the circus? Is there a bar there?'). The third answer is speed of reward. As I may have already said, no-one becomes addicted to a drug that works sometime next Thursday. This is why smoking is so popular (eight nicotine tours are completed around the brain within a minute of lighting up). The speed of punishment, however, is comparatively slow. HIV, liver disease, lung cancer, divorce, they're all miles away, over the horizon and out of sight. OK, so the rent's a month or two overdue, but the landlord's only in town on a Wednesday, so if I… Not only is punishment slow to come, with enough planning and evasion, it can be avoided altogether. Plus, it's tough out there. We may feel that we need a little something just to keep going.

> *It's like a jungle sometimes,*
> *It makes we wonder*
> *How I keep from going under.*
> Melly Mel and Grandmaster Flash, *The Message* (1982)

Nick Heather and Ian Robertson (1997) make the observation that if you live on the edge, it's impossible to share in the rewards of society. Enter chemical, or brain reward.

Brain reward and overdose

There is evidence that as we get older the brain reward system doesn't work as well. We don't get as excited as we used to by the good things in life. Perhaps this is related to the equal tendency among older people not to be so upset by life's difficulties. Whatever the reason, this reduction in the supply of 'goodies' available to us can be the cause of particular frustration to someone whose life has become intimately involved with this area of the way we function. Addicts respond to this thorny problem with characteristic single-mindedness. They drink more, or take more drugs. Raising the stakes like this can pay off, but the health risks climb. Drug overdoses, which are distressingly common in the early years of drug misuse, become a real danger again among drug addicts in their thirties and over, particularly when additional drugs are thrown into the pot (European Monitoring Centre for Drugs and Drug Addiction [EMCDDA], 2000). Almost 30% of Italian injecting drug addicts, for instance, are dead before they reach 40 (Davoli *et al*, 1997), and it's rare for anyone with this habit to make 50. It's too punishing to the body.

4
The addictive personality

People have been passing magnifying glasses over other people for the past two hundred years, looking for the missing or extra bits that make up the addictive personality. They've had little luck so far (Schuckit *et al*, 1994a). We're all different in my town and the community of alcoholics and drug addicts seems to be equally varied.

Researchers measure personality by asking pre-set questions, sometimes called personality inventories. It's impossible to capture something as unique and complex as a human personality with a couple of sheets of A4 paper and a biro. Such psychological questionnaires can only establish a type or category of personality to which we could be said to belong. I've met a lot of people in my life, and I've never naturally arranged any of them by personality type in my mind. The nearest I've got to this are two lists headed, 'People I like' and 'People I don't'. I suspect most psychologists don't get any more systematic than this in their private lives. Even this method breaks down when people I don't like do something I approve of, or vice versa.

One of the main catch-all labels in psychiatry is a thing called antisocial personality disorder, or APD. It means someone who is reckless, usually male, bad at keeping to the law, lacks a sense of social responsibility, and is not brilliant at learning from bad experiences. A person with APD is not generally found among the membership of the Town's Women's Guild. There's a significant connection between antisocial personality disorder and drug and alcohol problems. A cynic might argue that a person with a diagnosis of personality disorder is simply someone who has fallen out with a psychiatrist. The label is certainly very broad – how many of us have a truly *ordered* personality?

Sufferers of APD are the only type of personality that researchers have consistently linked with addiction. This basically boils down to: people who behave badly often get drunk and/or stoned. They just don't care. From a large sample of Americans, Schuckit (1989) claimed that 70% of men with APD had had some form of alcohol problem in their lives. In 1993, Winters *et al* surveyed juvenile offenders. They calculated that half of this population had drug problems. I worked in a prison for a while, and from the best guesses of some of the inmates I talked to, 90% of the prisoners had drug or alcohol problems. But I also met a number of people who were far from the stereotype, including a tee-total burglar and a born-again Christian armed robber (he only robbed when he was poor, and was always polite).

We know enough about psychology now to see that evaluating a person's nature is a two-way thing. If a psychologist interviews us and we don't warm to him, we will give answers that reflect the uneasy mood that being in his company creates within us. A different psychologist, on another day, may elicit a totally different set of answers from us. The result? We officially become the proud owner of two separate personalities.

So what do people mean when they say, 'I know what I'm like. I've got an addictive personality'? Usually they're talking about their tendency to over-indulge in certain activities, like going to the gym, or eating cream cakes or smoking. All they're really saying is, 'I do more of some things than the majority of other people'. Part of our personality is about what we do, how we behave, but the fact that we do certain things doesn't necessarily tell us much about the person underneath. Science hasn't come up with too many answers about the internal factors that make some people prone to addiction. As I've indicated, this may be due to the inadequacy of current scientific methods, rather than the possibility that there is no such thing as an addictive personality.

So if we abandon science for a moment and delve into folk law, what are the more common elements of the addictive personality? A tendency towards obsession is one possibility. Unless you can genuinely concentrate your attention on taking a certain drug, it's unlikely that you are going to become successfully addicted to it. It has to dominate your thoughts. Nicotine and heroin may be exceptions: their extreme addictiveness makes it unnecessary to persistently keep them in mind. They do that for you.

To become addicted to a street drug we first have to break the law by getting hold of the stuff. Personal laws may also need to be broken. For instance, a person might promise himself not to drink again until the weekend, or not to score any more crack tonight, but they find that they can't keep their own rules. Viewed this way, addiction can be seen as a problem of breaking individual and social laws about chemicals: forbidden fruit. Addiction features weak personal boundaries, and these poor boundaries can extend to other areas of life. An addict can consent to sex with someone they don't really like, for instance, or get dragged into an argument that is none of their making. Some addiction watchers believe that this problem with rules comes from early learning experiences, including family life.

This idea about rule-breaking does not hold true for a number of alcoholics, who may be very solid – rigid almost – in their observance of social rules and laws. The alcoholic can be a deeply conventional person who only causes the eyebrows of others to rise when they notice exactly how many whiskies are being drunk. If he were shameless in his drinking he could perhaps be seen as a closet rebel, but many alcoholics take a fairly dim view of their own drunken behaviour.

A third possible component of an addictive personality is difficulty with tolerating emotions (Khantzian, 1985). I've heard it said several times that addicts are unusually sensitive people. I still can't decide whether this is the case, or if it's nearer to the truth to say that they're 'junkies and drunkies' in search of an excuse. To be fair, the history of art is crammed with the work of alcoholics and drug addicts: Colleridge, Wilde, Hemmingway, Lennon, Parker, Hendrix, Holliday. These people have come to be loved and admired because they have been able to express something deep and heartfelt within us. It's possible that the addict has emotions that are so strong that he or she needs a drink or a hit just to keep from going crazy. They're stuck on this perpetual helter-skelter, and any kind of relief is welcomed. It's not simply a desire for martyrdom that makes a long-suffering partner remain with an addict. The emotional pitch at which their life is lived can make an addict such exciting company that others can't help but come along for the ride. And, like the addict, once they're on, they find it almost impossible to get off.

An addict can be deeply sensitive toward his or her own feelings, but staggeringly insensitive to the feelings of those around them. It's not that the addict doesn't care – at other times he or she can be among the most attentive and considerate people you could hope to meet – it's more that they suffer from intermittent personal blindness ('Why are you so upset? We can always have a holiday next year'). This ability of an addict to upset loved ones without realising it causes the addict considerable confusion. They genuinely can't see what all the fuss is about, and it distresses them to see someone they care about so distraught.

Alternatively, this sensitivity could be nothing more than a convenient red herring. An alcoholic told me that he would sometimes engineer a row between his wife and himself, at the height of which he would shout something like, 'That's it, I'm not going to be mistreated like this!', and charge out of the house and straight down the pub. He'd plan this event hours ahead. His wife would be left holding the baby, and all the negative feelings that he couldn't handle – fear, anger and hurt.

If there really is such a thing as an addictive personality, impulsiveness has to be its most common feature. I've met quite a few ponderous, measured citizens with serious addictions, but I believe I've come across more impetuous addicts. McGue *et al* (1997) found some evidence that alcoholics were poor at self-restraint. We probably didn't need a team of psychologists to work that one out, but it's nice when real life and science agree. Doing things on impulse is almost bound to be related to addiction. This impulsiveness could be an inborn characteristic of addicts, or a sign that some people can't bear to unwind, let go and stop reacting to what's around them.

The fourth and last contender for the addictive personality missing link title is good old-fashioned self-centredness. Addicts can be very sensitive to their own needs, but less highly tuned to the needs of those around them. Maybe the preoccupation of addiction doesn't permit any time to focus on others, or maybe they're too out of it to focus on much at all.

There's a school of thought that says rather than being too selfish, the addict is too selfless, taking on the worries and responsibilities of others, or acting as the one who has to be happy and positive. This sort of addict believes that whatever he or she takes on, they'll be alright. They'll cope. They can't so they don't cope, but it's hard for the addict or their loved ones to see a connection between putting too much strain on inner resources and then emotionally refuelling with chemicals.

The selfishness idea is too simplistic really. I think with addiction it's more a case of self-absorption. The addict is busily engaged in finding the right balance between taking a drug (eg. alcohol) and sustaining a happy life. As the drug intake goes up, the happy life becomes harder to attain, but the addict finds it difficult to make a link between these two factors. It can't be the drug, because it's the drug that helps them to be happy. It must be something else. The addict goes through a mental inventory. 'Is it the house? I never did like living in this town. I don't know why we moved here in the first place. And that job's driving me nuts. The kids are just plain ignorant half the time, and all Tina can do is nag me rotten about stupid little things. I tell you, I could do with a drink'. No one seems to understand how hard the addict is trying. The addict doesn't seem to understand how his life is being made miserable through his relationship with a drug. He seems selfish enough, but he's probably no more selfish than the rest of us who make it their aim in life to be happy. He's just looking in the wrong places, and the harder he searches… As someone wise once said, when you find yourself in a whole, the first thing to do is to stop digging.

Addiction and crime

I've met a great many addicts and a reasonable number of them have maintained pricey drug habits without recourse to burglary, theft, or fraud. Others have slipped from the straight and narrow, but if you are seeking out and taking potent illicit drugs, exactly how near to the middle of the straight and narrow were you in the first place? You're already a criminal by virtue of the top item on your shopping list.

Robert Cloninger (1987) (see *p.48*) was right – many drug addicts are characters with a talent for breaking society's rules. They have their own moral code. If it matches the law of the land then great, but this may often be as a result of coincidence rather than a desire on the part of the addict to conform. Someone with a drug problem may have been light-fingered before he or she got addicted to anything more expensive than Marlboro's.

Crime in its own curious way is a bit of a drug. The adrenaline thrill of defying your fears and breaking in somewhere in the dead of the night can lighten up many a tedious week. Add to this the possibility of ready cash, and we can begin to see why our local constabularies have their work cut out. Young offenders often talk about the 'buzz' they get from committing crime, and it's often a quest for sensation, rather than the dough, that draws them into conflict with the law. One bloke told me that he only began to get excited by a criminal activity when he could hear the sound of approaching police sirens. Another lad I met had made it his habit to steal cars and take them straight to the doorstep of the local police station, where he would perform tyre-squealing pirouettes until the officers inside would put down their sandwiches and mugs of tea and give chase. It's a little astonishing that this young man would want to risk his liberty for nothing more profitable than a good laugh, but not much more astonishing perhaps than the chances alcoholics and drug addicts take with their lives in pursuit of something similar. It would seem that a good laugh is hard to beat.

Ultimately, hopefully, we all grow up. The joy-rider finds

himself with a family to keep, and the getting of money rather than a fun night out becomes his priority. His criminal activities become more professional and profit-orientated and less playful. Or he may have developed a nasty little drink or drug habit and, again, cash becomes a necessity. The economic pressure created by addiction can make a criminal of relatively law-abiding citizens. Shoplifting and fraud are two common activities for these reluctant but desperate individuals. The internal conflict and anxiety caused by engagement in activities that are alien to his or her nature can be almost intolerable to this kind of person. Extreme nervousness coupled with a lack of professional aptitude often result in arrest and even imprisonment.

These unfortunate cases are more rare than those of the habitual law-breaker who also happens to have an addiction problem. Stereo-typically he is in his mid-twenties, has around twenty previous convictions for a variety of offences, and is something of an opportunist or all-rounder, having burgled, stolen cars, defrauded, dealt in stolen goods and so on. Addiction influences his criminal activity in terms of the frequency of his crimes. He needs plenty of money. Edmunds *et al* (1998) estimated that 'problem drug users' cost this country up to £2.5 billion per year as a result of theft.

It is no coincidence that the man responsible for addressing drug problems in the UK is a former Chief Police Constable.

One addict told me that he had been using £200 worth of drugs a day. He'd wake up each morning with 50 pence in his pocket. The next few hours would be spent ripping off some unsuspecting person or two and selling their possessions on until he had the necessary two hundred. He'd spend it all on drugs, crash out, and wake up the following morning with 50 pence in his pocket. The next few hours would be spent… Whether it was the same coin or not I forgot to ask, but this lifestyle did have a poetic symmetry to it.

The final and most obvious area of criminal activity involving chemical addiction is drug dealing. One surefire way of affording a drug habit is to buy the stuff in bulk and sell it on in smaller amounts to other drug users. The profit generated pays for the addict's personal consumption. He or she now has free drugs and plenty of new 'friends'. It's an attractive but risky option, with capture resulting in almost certain imprisonment.

Unreliability and a tendency to consume some of the retail stock as well as their cost-free personal allowance prevent addicts from moving up the drug-dealing ladder to become wholesalers, distributers and importers. These profitable positions are usually occupied by *bona fide* criminals who are addicted to money, not drugs.

5
Alcohol

Alcohol and biology

Alcohol and the brain

How does alcohol work? How do we get drunk? It's not too simple really, but it's a lot to do with a chemical called gamma-aminobutyric acid, or GABA for short. We all naturally produce GABA, and it is closely involved in the transmission of messages through the brain. GABA doesn't push these messages through. Instead, it acts a little like a brake, slowing them down, calming the brain's hectic communication network. Alcohol increases this damping down effect of GABA.

Two of the main signals GABA helps to moderate are anxiety and coordination. So if we drink a lot we relax but fall over.

In addition to being untroubled and fairly unsteady, alcohol can also make us feel excited, by increasing the flow of the hormone noradrenaline (adrenaline's equally hyperactive sister) through the brain. So we move around for no particular reason and talk mainly drivel. Too much of this can be difficult for the rest of us to take, but the alcoholic often has the good fortune not to be listening at the time, as a full load of these two brain chemicals (GABA and nor-adrenaline) make concentration a bit of a lost cause. This impairment of concentration largely explains why drunks are so bad at driving.

Even if the alcoholic had been listening, he or she may not remember what they've said anyway. This is because alcohol messes up bits of the brain called NMDA receptors. NMDA performs a vital role in recording what happens in our lives. Put simply, it's a memory chemical. Serious drinking can disable our memory functioning for hours or even days. An alcoholic woman told me that one day she'd found herself walking down a street on the Costa Brava. This surprised her, as her last conscious memory had been of sitting in a pub in Birmingham. Some Midlandists might view this as a potentially beneficial side-effect of alcohol, but they should be aware that an unknowing journey in the opposite direction is an equal danger once enough 'cuda libras' have been sunk.

What is eerie about these lost weekends is that all the while the drinker appears to have his wits about him and is capable of perfectly rational and spontaneous conversation. What is not apparent is that none of what is happening is 'going in'. I've had quite involved chats with drinkers as they've been drying out, talking to them on two or three separate occasions over the course of a working week. By Friday I've gone to speak with them again, satisfied by now that they really quite like me, only to be greeted with a blank expression and the question, 'I'm sorry but who are you?' I prefer to blame faulty NMDA transmission rather than any personality deficit on my part.

This temporary amnesia is quite different from the kind of ongoing short-term memory loss that can result from years of sustained boozing. This tragic condition resembles senile dementia or Alzheimer's disease. It's caused by permanent damage to a critical percentage of the brain's stock of three trillion cells, and is largely irreversible.

When it comes down to just feeling good, alcohol makes us produce and then propel the chemical dopamine along the brain reward pathway, the mind's own motorway of pleasure. Alcohol also pushes up our stocks of serotonin, the deliriously happy brain chemical which is the primary target of the drug ecstasy. It's probably serotonin that is to blame for a drunk person's irritating tendency to drawl how much they love you.

There's one more way in which alcohol makes itself attractive to drinkers. Sjoquist *et al* (1982) dissected the brains of dead alcoholics (you'll have to ask him why) and saw that they had been structurally changed in a way very similar to the brains of some heroin addicts. No-one is quite sure what's going on here, but alcohol seems to tap in to a bit of that same wiring circuit which is the target for heroin and other opiates. This may explain some of alcohol's pain-killing properties, and it's capacity to give the drinker an opium sense that all's well with the world, despite the fact that he's utterly skint, his marriage is at an end, and he's just about to get the sack.

Alcohol is certainly good at creating a sense of calm and control, but this point of satisfaction has been reached by some kind of liquid trick. More than re-visiting the pub each night, the alcoholic has been trying to perpetually re-occupy his or her own castle in Spain. The real situation makes itself all too apparent the following morning. Fortunately, the true addict has just the answer: drink more. Some people do so as soon as they can reach an arm out from under the duvet. Others decide to tough it out till the evening. The binge drinker may recuperate for days, then hit the stuff again with renewed enthusiasm.

When it comes to doling out pleasure, the brain is a fairly generous organ, but it's not bloody stupid. We might have gained fantastic neural reward the first time we caught sight of ourselves in a blue velvet jacket, but two decades later the magic fades. To keep on drinking or taking drugs, year in, year out, and expect to feel the same elation that the stuff created during our teenage years is to fly in the face of common sense. In 1985 many people judged that thoroughly highlighted hair and a shell suit were just the things to bring sophistication into their lives. Few still hold this belief.

The problem is mainly one of tolerance. After just one drug experience our brains begin to adjust to having alcohol or amphetamine swimming around inside of us. To take the case of alcohol, we then have to drink more to get the same effect. Our brains respond by becoming more resistant to alcohol. How this comes to happen is far from clear. Scientists have caringly engaged in the slaughter of thousands of inebriated rats in the pointless pursuit of this question. So as not to encourage the murder of any species that's unlikely to develop an off-licence system, I'll just say that we are designed to resist mental confusion. We do this by mapping out any new world we find ourselves in, learning how to navigate our way through its alien landscape. After a few visits we barely feel like strangers – we become accustomed and acclimatised to Alcoworld. This is exactly what the dedicated drinker doesn't want, so once again he increases his intake. The brain resists further. The whole thing gradually builds up like some teetering pile of Jenga bricks. Things are now looking less than sound.

Metabolism

As alcohol is broken down in the body it is turned into a nasty chemical called acetaldehyde. One of the ways in which we digest alcohol is to produce stuff called ALDH, which attacks acetal-whatever-it's-called. If someone is lacking in ALDH, this acetaldehyde can build up, giving the unlucky drinker palpitations, a burning sensation in the stomach and a flushed face. This condition is known as Oriental Flush, as it's estimated that almost half of all Asians do not produce adequate ALDH. The result is that small amounts of alcohol make a sizeable proportion of Asia feel dog rough, so they are in no danger of becoming alcoholics. Strict cultural disapproval of drunkenness in many Asian communities also puts the brakes on the development of alcoholism (Schuckit, 1987).

Genetics

More about the brains of alcoholics

To clear the brain of old chemical messengers the brain uses a chemical called MAO. Abnormal levels of MAO in the brain can have an effect on our mood and our ability to concentrate. MAO is often a factor in serious depression. You can measure MAO levels in someone by taking a sample of their blood, and a number of studies claim to have found low MAO activity in the brains of alcoholics (Sullivan *et al,* 1987; Yates *et al*, 1990) and even the sons of alcoholics (Scher, 1983). It's possible that alcohol can have a lasting detrimental effect on someone's ability to be happy and to concentrate on doing things that might make him or her happier still. In a small number of people it appears that this damage can be passed on to the next generation.

Other enzymes (body agents that digest chemicals in the brain or elsewhere) are thought to be involved in the passing on of alcoholism through the family. In particular, one that is over-eager in eating up the happiness brain chemical serotonin has been found in the sons of alcoholic dads (Rausch *et al*, 1991).

So what does all this mean? After years of education I'm not sure I understand it myself, but I think I'm on safe ground if I say:

1.   The way our brains respond to alcohol may be different to other people's if our ancestors drank to extremes.
2.   This altered way of responding can mean that the offspring of alcoholics (and perhaps drug addicts) are more likely to have problems of poor concentration and low mood. This balance might be corrected by fairly heavy drinking or even drug-taking.

So can't something be done? As has often been the case in addiction, the answer to a problem with a drug has been the offer of another. In this event problem drinkers have been given antidepressants on the basis that they've possibly been drinking to sort out some mental gloominess. Has this worked? There is some evidence of success coming from America (Naranjo *et al*, 1987), where it's not unusual for doctors to prescribe these tablets for people with drink problems, but generally, antidepressants haven't been the answer. I've met plenty of alcoholics who drink freely on them.

Brainwaves

There's another way in which the brain may be disrupted by the influence of genes. For example, you're out for a walk and you know that an unusual bird sometimes nests in the area. You turn a corner and there it is, the Lesser Spotted Woodpecker! Our brain registers the image of the bird and after approximately 300 milliseconds it generates a positive electrical signal. This electrical pulse is known as the P300 wave, and it's a natural response to unusual but anticipated sights or sounds. This P300 wave is significantly smaller in around one third of the sons of alcoholic fathers (Begleiter *et al*, 1984). Does this mean that if your dad drank too much you probably won't take up bird spotting? No, but what the P300 story does tend to show is that the brains of some people with alcoholism in their families work slightly differently to your standard 'off-the-shelf' grey matter.

So we have a way of identifying people who may be at risk of developing alcoholism. Wire them up and measure their brainwaves. What should we do? One current idea is testing and counselling for children. They'd be told, 'Look, our tests show that you may be at risk of becoming an alcoholic. Stay away from drinking and do something else instead'. Sounds a bit tough, particularly if you live in my town.

There's been some evidence that the amount of cigarettes people smoke may be related to the smoking of their biological parents, beyond the simple influence that they saw their mum or dad wandering around with a cigarette for much of their childhood (Pedersen, 1981). These are early days, scientifically speaking, but it now seems that vulnerability to addiction to a number of drugs other than alcohol can be genetically handed down.

So, what happens when someone from a family with a history of alcoholism actually takes a drink? Well, compared to someone from a relatively 'dry' family, there is virtually no difference in the rate at which the alcohol builds up in the blood stream, and in the peak concentration of alcohol in the blood that they both eventually reach. In other words, the same amount of alcohol gets into their systems. After this point things change. When asked how they feel after they've had a standard quantity of alcohol, a man or woman from an 'alcoholic' family usually score the effects lower than someone from the non-alcoholic family. They don't seem to be as drunk (Schuckit, 1989; Lex *et al*, 1988). People from alcoholic families also tend to sway less when asked to stand rigidly still after having a drink, almost as if they have been genetically pre-programmed not to spill their pint.

By not registering the full impact of alcohol in his or her blood stream, a person from a family with a history of alcoholic drinking may continue knocking them back. It's sometimes said of someone with a drink problem that, 'He doesn't seem to know when he's had enough'. It may be nearer the heart of the matter to say that he needs to have more to get to the point where he's had enough. Unfortunately, alcohol has a broad range of influences over how we function mentally, emotionally and physically, and a vital line can be crossed between safety and danger in the pursuit of the state of 'enough'.

Alcohol and the profile of a typical drinker

The Swedes have a nasty alcohol problem, and being a socially responsible people, they have been desperate to crack the riddle of addiction. Copenhagen has the largest library on alcoholism in the world, and a lot of precise and painstaking investigation has been done, but many Swedish citizens continue to drink with worrying Scandinavian thoroughness.

One of the best ideas to have come out of the Swedish alcohol studies has been that of Robert Cloninger (1987). Using his own questionnaire to measure certain character traits of problem drinkers, Cloninger concluded that there were two types of alcoholics. The first type don't really start drinking properly until the age of 25. They are passive people who don't like a lot of hassle, are not particularly spontaneous, and tend to obey the law. Type 1 alcoholism does not appear to be inherited.

Type 2 alcoholics are the complete opposite. They are almost always male, heavy drinkers from an early age, less passive, more impulsive and thrill-seeking, and much more likely to be involved in crime. Type 2 alcoholism could well be inherited and may jump a generation.

There appears to be a fair bit of truth in Cloninger's way of looking at alcoholism, and it applies quite well to drug addiction as well, but a number of drinkers and drug-takers don't fit neatly into either one camp or the other, as Irwin *et al* (1990) found out when they tested the idea on a group of alcoholics.

Some lines of work are more likely to produce addictions than others. Journalists, dentists, doctors and (of course) workers in the leisure and entertainment industry are more prone to addiction problems than the average citizen. It appears to be related to opportunity and irregular working hours. The opportunity comes with working alone and unsupervised, and sometimes in the presence of large quantities of alcohol. Whether the job makes the worker alcoholic, or the alcoholic naturally gravitates towards the kind of job where they can drink in peace is almost impossible to know. Alcoholics are rarely postmen (DeLint and Schmidt, 1971). Presumably, getting up early is a considerable hurdle, and the daily prying eyes of hundreds of customers can bring a promising career to a rapid end, particularly if you fall off your bike.

Alcohol and families (genetic)

As I've already mentioned, children of alcoholics are far more likely to become alcoholic than children of non-alcoholic parents (Schuckit, 1987). In Denmark, Goodwin (1979) looked at the sons of alcoholics. According to his figures, these children were four times more likely to become alcoholics than the sons of non-alcoholic parents. This four to one proportion held true, even when the sons were adopted and brought up by relatively sober surrogate parents. Maybe the trauma of being adopted drove the poor lads to drink? Or perhaps their new mum and dad were really mean to them, causing the sort of distress you'd like to chemically escape? Apparently not, since these boys didn't develop the other kinds of mental problems which you would expect from these types of experiences (such as anxiety, depression, delinquency and hyperactivity) to nearly the same proportion as their alcoholic drinking.

So it's genetic then, addiction? Case solved. Well it's surprising stuff and certainly makes you think. Alcoholism runs through some families like freckles. I was recently talking to the parents of four-year-old Danny, who looked strikingly similar to his granddad. 'He even has his grandad's temper', they told me. 'And he already loves a drink', added his mum. Grandad's alcoholism was common knowledge. In his short life Danny had seen little of his granddad. We three adults, sensing the presence of thirsty DNA and a potentially bad story waiting to unfold, fell silent. We changed the subject as soon as it could appear that the subject wasn't being changed.

This genetic weakness or susceptibility to alcoholism probably has something to do with the structure of the brain of descendents of alcoholic ancestors (Blum *et al*, 1990). We have a number of areas of the brain that respond to the pleasure chemical dopamine (see *Chapter 3, p.33*). Offspring of alcoholic families tend to have an important physical difference in the parts of certain brain cells. These affected areas are known as the dopamine D2 receptors. It's complicated if you're not a brain surgeon, but the bottom line on all this is that generations of heavy drinking can cause abnormalities in the brains of children to come. These offspring will have brains which are primed to expect alcohol. Comings *et al* (1994) found evidence that someone with abnormal D2 receptors has a greater risk of becoming a drug addict as well as an alcoholic. People he studied with this funny D2 receptor spent on average twice as much on drugs as other folk, and were apparently more violent.

6

The stimulants: amphetamines, cocaine and crack

Amphetamines

This chemical was first made in the early twentieth century and was used by doctors for a number of problems from depression to obesity. Amphetamine is now almost exclusively a street drug, made in back-street laboratories from relatively cheap ingredients. It is commonly called speed, which says it all. People are accelerated on amphetamine, moving and talking almost incessantly and to almost no purpose. The purpose, of course, is that speed makes people feel good. It does this by getting the brain to release unusually high amounts of dopamine, the chemical that has a central role in the brain pleasure circuits. Amphetamine also pushes up the quantity of noradrenaline in the users brain, causing him or her to be hyper-awake, hyperactive and hyper-vigilant. Amphetamine can also instruct the brain to release serotonin, which is very nice too.

Amphetamine puts the heart through a tough time, making it beat faster and harder. A friend of mine decided to give amphetamine a miss when one of the random thoughts that it generated in his speeding mind was that we only have so many heartbeats in a lifetime. The drug ate up a week's worth of his life as he paced around, desperately trying to work out a way of slowing the mad tick of his life-clock.

Speed addicts don't eat much. The noradrenaline kills the appetite stone dead. Amphetamine also weakens the gums and lets in decay. A hard-core speed addict will often have teeth that resemble a row of condemned houses. When offered chocolates, he will probably go for the soft centres. Sooner or later, though, every one of us must eat. To the speed addict this can be an awkward and alien necessity. And a waste of good drug money.

A friend told me that he had been chatting with Nick, his neighbourhood speed addict. This energetic but worryingly narrow man suddenly stopped talking. When this happens to an amphetamine addict you can be sure that something serious is going on, such as death. 'Oh no!' he said, 'I've just remembered, Terry's due round my place about now, and I've left a tin of dog food in the cupboard!' With that he bolted home. Terry was the town's other leading speed addict, and the dog food promised enough calories for a good few days' of speeding. Next time my friend bumped into Mick he asked him how the dog food panic had finished up. 'I was too late', lamented Nick, 'Terry had been round and he'd had the bloody lot'. Now not everyone who sniffs a line of speed is going to end up squabbling over tins of Pedigree Chum (Nick had standards, after all), but this strangely unnerving story does illustrate how our priorities can shift if we find something more important to us than anything that's gone before. He'd probably flogged the cooker a while back anyway.

Speed addicts are always on the go, doing things with a tremendous concentration of effort which to the casual observer have no value whatsoever. The Nicks or Terrys of this world may spend hours or even days dismantling old stereos or TVs, arranging and rearranging the parts in a sequence of mystifying piles. For all this intense labour we can predict that: a) not a single functioning machine will result; and b) they'll keep all the bits and move quickly on to collect and work on some new all-night project like abandoned table lamp-collecting or building a better wardrobe.

Too much amphetamine and too little sleep can combine to drive the amphetamine user over the edge into temporary insanity or 'amphetamine psychosis'. The style of this madness depends on the individual nature of the user, and where he or she happens to be at the time. A city-dweller who had slipped into amphetamine psychosis told me that he had become convinced that there was an international conspiracy to assassinate him. He stayed up all day and night, watching the movement of everyone on his road from behind his bedroom curtain, keeping meticulous records of the number plates of every car that came and went. He was sure his life depended on this knowledge. The things people do for fun. Another amphetamine user, living in the more natural environment of the Scottish Highlands, had the less paranoid delusion that his cottage was full of sheep. After he finally got some sleep and came to his senses he was surprised to find himself in a totally sheep-free home, the floor filled with bowls of water that he had kindly put out to give his imaginary woolly friends a drink.

Enough is enough, and either growing madness, malnutrition, or both can force the amphetamine addict to stop using for a while. Sleeping, eating, lethargy and a horrible blackness are usually the themes of the days that follow. Feelings of depression can drag on, making the idea of going back on the speed dangerously attractive.

These black episodes can come and go for as long as nine months as the brain struggles to get back to a normal level of chemistry (Gawin and Ellinwood, 1988).

Speed is not a rich person's drug (Wada, 1994). It's cheap and rough-edged, and if you've had amphetamine psychosis once, and you stay loyal to the drug, a repeat episode is always a possibility.

Cocaine and crack

Leaves from the coca plant have been chewed by the inhabitants of the Andes for the past 4000 years. The Incas regarded the plant as a gift from the Gods, and many people who have tried cocaine would probably go along with that.

Coca leaves are around 0.5% cocaine, and 99.5% green stuff you can probably do without. To the scientific mind this ratio suggested room for improvement, and around 150 years ago a method was developed for extracting almost pure cocaine from coca leaves. And so began the Western world's problem of access to a refined mind-altering drug that's just too nice for its own good. Freud was one of the first influential Westerners to be seduced by cocaine. In 1884 he wrote an article entitled 'Uber Coca', which more or less translated to 'Coke is Brilliant'. He recommended it to just about anyone in general, and himself in particular. In a particularly less-than-clever moment Freud touted cocaine as a likely cure for drug addiction, and was soon able to get a close friend of his (I think it was Wilheim Fliess) off morphine and firmly on to the white miracle, thereby creating Europe's first coke addict.

Meanwhile, in America, John Pemberton was busy patenting a soft drink that was rich in cocaine. Coca-Cola was soon tremendously popular. Conspicuously popular in fact, and in 1903 cocaine was removed from the recipe. Public opinion turned against cocaine and within a few years it was banned in Europe and the USA.

Cocaine was trendy for a while in the 1920s, but as most people during that time appeared to be otherwise engaged in riveting ships hulls or turning mangles, it didn't gain mass appeal. It wasn't until the 1970s that coke made a real comeback. In the preceding decade it had been regarded by the hippies as a 'bad' drug, best left to the junkies, but a lot of that fear and stigma melted away as a new generation of affluent and agreeably shallow party animals took over. Coke was OK.

Cocaine can be made doubly strong by a relatively simple home chemistry process. The resulting crystal is the infamous crack. Unlike coke, crack burns very readily, and so delivers a rocket-fast high.

Cocaine: what it does

You may not be surprised to read that cocaine also acts directly on the reward circuits of the brain. It's a stimulant, but a more subtle one than amphetamine. Coke doesn't shower the brain with extra torrents of the smiley dopamine and speedy noradrenaline. Instead it just puts a plug in the drain, bathing the brain in a rising tide of these twin chemicals. A very nice effect, but fairly short-lived, leaving the user with the straightforward choice of tracking down another little package of paradise, or turning in for an early night with a copy of the *Daily Mail*. It's at moments like these that addiction makes it move.

One of the main attractions of cocaine is that it tells you that you are great. Many of us don't need a great deal of convincing, and cocaine is such a thorough ego-booster that it really puts the question of our personal magnificence beyond even the most unreasonable doubt. This sense of self-importance makes it natural for a coke user to believe that they know best. In trying to help a cocaine addict to defeat his or her habit, I've often met with a sympathetic smile and some helpful advice on the proper way to tackle therapy. To a coke head, running the planet is all in a day's work.

Coke's a sensual drug, and some users find it an ideal accompaniment to sex. Having the best of both worlds (ie. sex and drugs) can make the prospect of quitting about as attractive as a fortnight's holiday in Dungeness, but coke addiction is an expensive hobby: crack smokers can comfortably hoover up £400 plus per day. Apart from the wallet, coke can be a bit too demanding on the heart, bringing a risk of heart attack or of a stroke as a result of volcanic blood pressure.

Lack of sleep, and the thorough wracking cocaine gives the user's poor brain, can do his/her mental health no favours. Paranoia is a common problem, creating the dilemma faced by many coke addicts of leaving the stuff alone (in which case what goes up soon comes crashing down), or smoking/sniffing some more, pushing the over-stretched mind to the point of break-down. Sounds terrible, and it can be. Thankfully help is at hand in the form of heroin. The ever-popular addict strategy of curing a drug problem by adding another one has resulted in many coke/crack users becoming instantly freed from the twin threats of paranoia and instant depression, and slipping instead into a soothing, dreamless sleep. Try this a few times and you wake up a heroin addict as well. Time to go back to the drawing board and the ceaseless quest for the perfect balance of drugs, a kind of chemical tightrope walk.

Some coke users drink alcohol to take the edge off the hyped-up, strung-up state that can result from a sustained coke binge. They won't end up heroin addicts if they stick to this strategy, but accidents can happen. The cocktail of coke and booze was a major cause of driver death on the streets of New York in the 1980s (Marzuk *et al*, 1990). Not that coke users drink for purely medicinal purposes anyway. It gives you something to do while you're out on the town or in front of the telly. Plus it's easy to drink when you're on coke; the beer, wine slides down very readily, and you don't even feel that drunk. In fact, you can drink for hours and hours and talk for much of that time too, punctuating your blindingly witty conversation and soothing your overworked throat with frequent slugs of alcohol. It's a tremendously popular pastime among coke users. One large-scale American study of cocaine addicts calculated that 94% of them were also addicted to alcohol (Miller and Gold, 1989).

Of course it's not all one-way traffic. Alcoholics have been known to sniff a few lines of coke themselves to add a bit of sparkle to their evening. Pub culture in London has now broadened to allow cocaine use to brace all the liquid shifting. Younger drinkers (principally males) see nothing wrong with it, but the police have a different and slightly less liberal point of view. To keep their licences intact landlords have taken to removing all flat horizontal surfaces from the pub toilets, so washroom shelves are vanishing fast and the tops of cisterns are now pitched like porcelain roofs.

All that sniffing and drinking can still leave an addict feeling frustratingly unsatisfied. Smoking might help, and approximately nine out of every ten coke addicts smoke cigarettes and dope (Gfroerer and Brodsky, 1993).

Cocaine isn't physically addictive. People can stop using it any time they want to, which may not be too often at all. On the other hand, taking stimulants for any protracted period of time can be an exhausting business. The highs get harder to reach and the mind and body begin to plead for a break. Sooner or later the coke addict has to give it a rest.

As with amphetamine, the trouble with giving up is the sudden feeling of depression that can descend. It may pass within a week or two, but five minutes of desperation is long enough in my book. Things begin to even out after a long-overdue lie in. A person coming off coke can sleep for 24 hours or more, and this period, when the coke head plummets back to earth, is known as 'the crash'. Even after a good sleep, the cocaine addict can feel tired and low for three or four weeks after stopping. All the same, the coke user may have very little desire to resume taking the drug. You know when you've had enough, and the last thing he or she probably needs is more hyping up. With a month or two's break from coke, however, the addict may be more than willing to re-enter the fray. Because it's a stimulant, coke is a very tempting solution to boredom – once you've taken it something's bound to happen. Or at least that's the way it seems. Crack addicts can remain in one or two rooms for a couple of days, deeply occupied with smoking and just generally fiddling about.

When other people arrive and join the party, things can turn pretty hectic in relatively no time. Sex, money, ego, paranoia and agitation can make a dangerous mix, and for some people this kind of action is as addictive as crack itself.

Conditioning

The drug addict or alcoholic can click back into drug use for any number of reasons, internal (feeling low or angry, unsettled) or external (sight of a public house, the smell of someone 'lighting up'). In some way the nervous system, the mind and body's pilot, has been re-programmed by the years of chemical messages pouring in.

As evolved beings we are beautifully designed to respond to the dangers and rewards our environment may present. Drugs can move right in on this system and go straight to the top. For instance, the very word drug has the capacity to strike fear into the hearts of most parents, particularly when heard in conjunction with other words such as, daughter and court appearance in Bangkok: the association of these words with danger is firmly rooted in our minds. A positive chemical experience can turn someone's automatic response to the word drug on its head. Suddenly it means fetch. A drug user has the uncanny ability to identify at a glance a stranger with the same secret habit. This is born of necessity as the stranger may have more drugs and better quality ones too. In times of shortage, the possibility that the stranger may have any drugs at all makes him an important contact to make, as meeting him could bring its own rewards.

Back in the forties Wikler (1948) claimed that former opiate users were re-experiencing the symptoms of drug withdrawal when they were encouraged to talk about their drug-using memories. They sniffed and yawned, and their eyes began to water. This seemed to be a similar sort of reaction to the one the famous Russian scientist Ivan Pavlov observed in his dogs. Like all dogs, their mouths watered whenever they saw their food coming. A bell was rung as the food was brought out to them. Pavlov went on to just ring the bell, but the dogs salivated anyway, anticipating dinner. Sadly we're no smarter when it comes to drug conditioning.

Craving

I don't know what I want, but I want it now.
Vivian Stanshall, Sir Henry at Rawlison's End, 1970

Craving is an uncomfortable state in which the sufferer becomes preoccupied with getting hold of the object of his or her desire. In addiction the most obvious example might be the shivering heroin addict who is desperate for some gear, or the shaky alcoholic who can't sleep for want of some Scotch. Neither of these cases, however, actually involve craving in its true meaning. They are both matters of straightforward physical withdrawal. If the heroin addict doesn't find any heroin for a few days, he will be:

- not very happy at all
- no longer physically addicted to heroin.

A similar situation arises for the drinker, although stopping drinking dead does involve a slight but real risk of an addicted person ending up exactly that, dead. But if we assume our alcoholic friend comes out the other side he may not want a drink. Let's face it, he's probably had enough just lately. Likewise, the heroin addict, no longer hooked on the stuff, may have no appetite for it. They are both now a long way from craving their particular poison.

No, craving is much more of a psychological kind of thing, triggered by a thought, or a smell or perhaps an image. It's probably fair to presume that you, dear reader, are not physically addicted to a particular type of cake. But say you're walking down the street and you pass the window of the best bakers in town, and you catch the aroma of baking just as a tray of the finest still-warm Danish pastries are being put out almost right under your nose. You alter course and sail straight up to the counter of that fabulous patisserie.

It's an impulsive thing. Supermarkets exploit this phenomenon by putting chocolate bars at the check out, waiting for us to crack under the strain of our own or our children's desire for a quick sugar hit.

Are either of these two examples of craving? I'd like to say yes, but the proper answer is, again, no. We went for the cake and the chocolate bar because we fancied them at the time. It was an almost automatic thing. If we had made it a few steps pass the shop, or to the sliding supermarket doors without weakening, the chances are that we wouldn't have then turned back.

But say we got home, put our feet up and began to brood on the delicious iced symmetry of that pastry, or the sweet sensation of the chocolate bar breaking between our teeth, and the more we tried to shut these visions out of our minds the stronger and more insistent they became, until we could all but taste the rich almond... well, you get the general idea.

Craving is a nagging, grinding kind of obsession, urging the craver to do what he doesn't want to do. A preoccupation with an object, or an activity.

Craving, in the addiction meaning of the word, can also occur when we've had a little bit of what we fancy and are trying to resist having any more. Laberg and Ellersten (1987) gave 16 'dry' alcoholics a small cocktail; it's probably not the most responsible gift you can give an alcoholic, but no doubt they were grateful. Next they hooked them up to some machines and showed them a second beverage. What these wacky scientists hadn't told the alcoholics was that only half of the drinks were alcoholic; the other half were alcohol-free. The alcoholics who had drunk the alcohol showed more activity in their nervous systems than those who had been given the dud (placebo) drink. The alcohol had whetted the appetites of those who'd drunk it.

Large-scale cocaine users often report that just the thought of the drug is sometimes enough to trigger an unsettling episode of craving. A sense of excitement, clamminess and the taste of coke forming in the back of the throat are common craving experiences. The physical signs of cocaine craving have been measured in a laboratory setting, with drug-free cocaine addicts being shown videos of their favourite powder (Childress *et al*, 1988). As viewing progressed the addicts' skin temperature dropped steeply, by 10°F or more.

Other researchers have found that alcoholics whose eyes literally widened at the sight of a drink (that's to say their pupils dilated) were more likely to relapse than alcoholics who had not shown this reaction (Kennedy, 1971). A similar picture emerged when smokers who had given up were taken into a laboratory, wired up to a heart monitor and shown a packet of cigarettes. Some of the volunteers showed a sharp drop in heart rate – a typical kind of 'craving' reaction. People in this group went back to smoking at a far higher rate than those whose pulses hadn't slowed (Niaura *et al*,1989).

The work of Kennedy and of Niaura seems to suggest that addiction can create an automatic physical reaction in a person which would make going back to drink or drugs a distressingly easy thing to do. Both researchers asked their volunteers how the sight of the alcohol or cigarettes made them feel. The answers did not tie up with whether they subsequently fell off the wagon or not. But, their physical responses did tend to predict this happening. Why is this so? It would seem that these physical changes represent the body preparing for the effects of the drug and going in the opposite direction to soften the impact. For instance, the skin temperature of opiate addicts has been found to drop just before they received an injection of their favourite kind of drug. This would prime them for the sudden warming effect of the drug. When they were jabbed with a dose of something that they were told was not an opiate, but in fact was, the volunteers' skin temperature climbed, presumably to prepare the body for the introduction of something that might be unpleasant (Ehrman *et al*, 1992).

On the surface, if we start to feel colder, our hearts beat slower, our mouths fill with saliva and we find ourselves sniffing and yawning, we might worry about our current state of health, take some Vitamin C and turn in for an early night. The drug addict or alcoholic, however, might have a far happier association with these sensations, actually relishing a cold shiver as he or she unwraps some promising-looking package, or licking their lips as they reach for a chilled pint of lager.

Whether this proves that craving can come from tasting what you want is uncertain. To go back to the cake shop again (hopefully for the last time), the cake was made all the more attractive by the smell of its baking. When we smell something we are effectively tasting it, as microscopic particles are drifting up our nose, exciting our nervous system. A 'priming' dose of alcohol may therefore amount to no more than a drift pass the pub's open door.

Craving tends to occur most frequently and most vigorously in the days and weeks that follow an addict giving up drink or drugs. A large chunk of life just isn't there any more, and as creatures of habit we tend to repeat a lot of things we do, and as sensitive beings we tend to pine what we have just lost, be it a faithful old car, an intimate relationship or a loyal pet. Time heals and we move on, but if something or someone has had a profound effect on our lives, then grieving can return a long way into the future. The problem with drugs, of course, is that you can bring them back. Research varies a little when it comes to what percentage of people who go back to addiction do so because they craved the drugs they left behind. Marlatt (1978) had probably got it right when he said that 5% of alcoholics and drug addicts went back into addiction due to craving.

Crack cocaine is perhaps the drug which former drug users crave more than any other. Just the sight of a standard disposal cigarette lighter was enough to set one addict I've known into a spin of thoughts and desire to take the drug again. That said, in a survey of crack users who had gone back to their pricey habit (Wallace, 1989), only 5.7% of those interviewed said that craving had been the reason for their slip.

Dope

Most experts believe that dope isn't addictive and most dope smokers tend to agree. But they get a bit twitchy when they run out. Cannabis is a borderline drug when it comes to addiction. It's officially a hallucinogenic, which means that rather than making you merry or excited, it makes things a bit strange, paranoic even. Each to their own, but as strangeness and paranoia are not two of the most obvious aspects of pleasure, it's a bit surprising that dope is consistently the most popular illicit drug across the UK and the rest of Europe.

But a lot of people just love weed. It has the capacity to make us giggle, mellow us out, and enhance our enjoyment of everything from food (provided we've got enough in the house) to sex (provided we can keep concentrating). Day-time TV chat shows featuring second-division ventriloquists, or 24-hour cable shopping channels become the most profound and dazzling achievements of civilisation within minutes of sparking up some decent 'skunk'. The stoned viewer becomes entranced by the screen, unable to move for fear of missing a single second of whatever electronic wallpaper is on at the time. Which is just as well because the hapless hippy a) can't exactly remember how to move and b) can't see the point anyway.

This 'why bother?' characteristic of dope has ruined an entire generation of promising young Brits. Until they got in to cannabis, many of today's youth were hungry for a life of professional and personal triumph, and all the glamorous rewards such achievements could bring. A year or two of solid dope-smoking and their only surviving ambition is to make a cup of tea. But who's going to go out and get the milk? The only time they leave the flat in 12 months is to go to their mum's or Glastonbury. The experts are right, cannabis isn't addictive as such. It's just that dope smokers can't be bothered to give it up. Or perhaps its the same old addiction story – if it changes how you feel, why not take it?

Bell *et al* (1997) surveyed 17,000 American students to ask about cannabis. Smokers tended to smoke cigarettes, binge drink, have multiple sexual partners, and look on parties as more important than church or community events. They didn't seem desperate to be rescued from their misery.

There are some people who actually thrive on dope, flying around town with a pipe and a lump of hash, stopping long enough for a smoke and a chat before charging off somewhere else. They may be pretty hooked on the stuff, but its relatively inexpensive and not too difficult to find, so it can be a benign addiction but for the fact that smoking anything heavily is never going to be good for the lungs or the heart or several other body parts. It's not too good for the head either, although the old idea that cannabis can drive you mad (ie. 'Reefer Madness') was pretty thoroughly disproved following examinations of long-term pot smokers from India (Chopra and Chopra, 1939) and Morocco (Benabud, 1957). What dope can do, however, is upset the mental balance of someone suffering from a serious mental illness such as schizophrenia. It has also been linked with depression and suicide (Dawson, 1998).

If there is such a thing as dope addiction, then the people who suffer from it tend to be vague, cagey to the point of paranoia, and remote. This remoteness or distance may be the result of spending too much time drifting about in inner space like some lost astronaut. But perhaps this zoned-out manner is not simply the cumulative effect of too many joints. Maybe to find twisting your head all day every day an appealing activity you have to be a bit unusual in the first place.

Dope lives on in the system for hours or days after a joint is smoked. An American study (Yesavage *et al*, 1985) found that pilots were still affected by a single joint 24 hours after stubbing it out.

They were put in a flight simulator, and they managed to take off and fly OK, but they tended to crash the thing when attempting to land, an important aspect of their work.

Dawson (1998) found evidence that alcohol and every street drug can promote physical aggression. The sole exception was, of course, dope. But whose turn is it to get the milk?

7

Nicotine

Cigarettes are the number one cause of drug death in the world. 120,000 UK citizens die every year from a smoking-related disease. 400,000 Americans go the same way. Given the monumental risks, why doesn't everyone give up? It can't be because cigarettes give us such an incredible 'high'. They don't. Any positive effect is subtle. So are people willing to risk their necks for subtlety? Obviously not. The main reason appears to be that nicotine is more addictive than anything else we can do in public. Just about everyone who smokes is hooked. Over 80% of smokers smoke every day (Pierce *et al*, 1997). Now that can't be a matter of choice, with the smoker waking up and thinking, 'This is an ideal day for smoking approximately 25 cigarettes – lucky me.' Most smokers want to wake up and not smoke.

The second factor in people smoking themselves to death is one of distance from the problem. We all know that it can take years off your life, but that's a long way off. Long enough for it to have little emotional impact on us. We don't get scared about what may happen 20 years or so down the line. Why bother? We've got enough hassle right now what with relationship problems, aggro at work, the car playing up, money worries… anyone seen my fags?

We're too close to nicotine to see how bizarre and dangerous a habit it is. For what other reason would we allow near strangers to repeatedly set fire to things in our own homes? And how could it be that a daft habit should have been allowed to kill so many people in the terrible fires at Kings Cross and Bradford?

To understand the power of nicotine, we need to look back. Colombus's log from his first journey to the Americas records the discovery of tobacco. Colombus described how the native Caribs 'drank smoke' (there was no verb 'to smoke' in European vocabulary at that point), and he went on to add that his men had been very keen to return to the island the next day for another go at this strange leaf. Addiction didn't lose time. The exploding popularity of this new drug across the world caused joy, anger and panic. In 1615 the chief of the English factory in Hirado, Japan wrote:

> *The King has ordered no tobacco to be drunk in his government… It is strange to see how these Japanese men,*

women, and children, are besotted in drinking that herb;
and not ten years since it was first in use.

Brooks, 1953

He couldn't have known that the same thing was happening all over Europe at the same pace. In 1634 the Czar of Russia introduced corporal punishment for tobacco smokers. Persistent offenders were to be executed. The death sentence was brought to Japan, Persia and India too, for tobacco possession and dealing. A public announcement made in seventeenth century Sicily that the tobacco on the island had been poisoned (tobacco was cut with all sorts of things in those days) failed to stop many smokers from taking a mad risk by continuing to puff.

James I, who famously detested tobacco, did the craftier British thing and decided to make a fortune out of the stuff. He increased the duty on tobacco by a ludicrous 4,000%, and – of course – people paid up, because they were already hooked. Either that, or they turned to the smuggling trade, which became vast. Walpole tried to introduce stricter laws on tobacco, but he backed off when faced with a violent uprising. As recently as Gorbachov's period of office as Soviet president, there were civil disturbances in a number of Russian cities when cigarette manufacture could not keep pace with demand (Sosnov, 2000). No one could stop nicotine and no one has. Even Adolf Hitler, who despised tobacco, realised that he didn't have the power to beat the stuff.

Putting aside the fact that they are unstoppable killers, cigarettes can be quite soothing, and we can smoke them without fear of losing our ability to do things. We can smoke and think, smoke and talk and smoke and drive, although we need to be cautious when refuelling.

A group of smokers can in some subtle way be better company than a group of non-smokers. They're that bit more relaxed, less 'stiff'. Some of this can be explained by the fact that they share the same habit. Smokers also tend to literally share their fags, creating a convivial, if carcinogenic, atmosphere. But there may be another influence at work. This is related to the emotional circuits of the brain. Two of the emotions that seem to be most closely involved with nicotine are anger and fear. Before a nerve-wracking event like an interview or a court appearance, smokers will tend to smoke more heavily and more vigorously. They'll talk about feeling 'dead nervous' and 'needing a fag'. Likewise, if something has happened to upset or antagonise a smoker, he or she will probably light up almost straight away and smoke furiously. So smokers may be less up-tight than other people, until they run out of cigarettes or try to give up.

Nicotine is really a stimulant. It triggers the release of a number of chemicals around the body. These include adrenaline, noradrenaline and (of course) dopamine. But smokers often say that they smoke because it relaxes them. We don't know why this should happen – that nicotine appears to act as both a stimulant and a tranquilliser – it may be something to do with nicotine latching on to nerve cells across a very broad area of the brain. This relaxing effect could also be related to the presence of carbon monoxide in fags. This lethal gas makes us sleepy prior to it making us dead. I don't think it's possible to smoke enough cigarettes to effectively commit carbon monoxide suicide, but each puff could be damping down areas of the nervous system. A third possibility is that rather than acting as a tranquilliser, a cigarette may simply be stopping nicotine withdrawal. And the number one symptom of nicotine withdrawal is agitation. So having a fag equals no agitation equals calm.

If this third reason is true we might expect the first fag of the day to be particularly calming, as the smoker hasn't had a puff for eight hours. What actually happens is the opposite (West and Schneider, 1988) – it causes the smoker's heart to race, kick starting the day. Add a cup of coffee and you're soon awake, which I suppose is an explanation in itself: the smoker would have been agitated due to the low levels of nicotine in his blood, only he was too sleepy to get wound up about anything. Had he woken up and found his cigarette packet empty, we could predict that he'd quickly begin to experience the agitation of Benson withdrawal.

Another reason why nicotine is so popular is speed of effect. It is felt within eight seconds of ignition. Within the first minute eight waves of nicotine have washed through the brain. Regardless of how mild the pleasurable effects of cigarettes might be, their speed of delivery can make them hard to resist.

There's a common assumption among smokers that there comes a point when giving up is not going to save your health; you've been smoking for too many years and the damage is done. This opinion can be pretty depressing, but there is strong evidence that many health risks reduce relatively soon after stubbing out the last coffin nail, and improvement continues with the passage of time. The chances of getting lung cancer, or of having a heart attack are the same for an ex-smoker as they are for a hardly-smoked-at-aller within three to eight years of the ex-smoker giving up the habit (US Department of Health, 1990).

Jasinski *et al* (1984) injected volunteers with three separate solutions of amphetamine, morphine and nicotine. The volunteers were not told which drug was in which syringe. They were then asked to say which of the jabs they liked the best. Surprisingly, nicotine was rated as highly as the speed and the opiate, showing that it's capable of playing with the big boys in terms of pleasure. What was also interesting was the volunteers' tendency to smoke a cigarette after the jabs. This must have been more to do with automatic activity rather than a need for nicotine. Smoking's mad really.

Nicotine makes you sick when you first try it, and it can do the same to experienced smokers if they go silly on the stuff. But rather than smoking in a haphazard pattern, smokers are expert in unconsciously regulating and fine-tuning the amount of nicotine in their brains. Low tar cigarettes offer less nicotine, so smokers tend to pull much harder on this type of cigarette, extracting the full dose of nicotine (and tar, unfortunately) required.

It's true that nicotine can keep weight off people. It probably does this by reducing the appetite. It's a stimulant after all, distantly related to slimming pills, which are severe appetite killers. It also quickens the metabolism, burning up the calories. When people quit smoking these twin effects of nicotine – making a smoker eat less and burn up more food – are reversed. This makes it likely that someone who gives up will gain weight.

As well as food, nicotine quickens up the rate at which we digest other drugs (Benowitz, 1988), which may be a reason why people who are a bit worse for wear sometimes say, 'I'll just have a fag so I can get my head together'. Excellent idea.

The younger you are when you first smoke, the greater your chance of becoming addicted. Breslau *et al* (1993) calculated that if you keep away from tobacco until you are 17, you've made yourself a bit safer but, even so, it's not the best drug to play around with. Knowing how addictive and poisonous it is (nicotine is actually a primary ingredient in many insecticides) is no protection. A study in Equador, for instance, found that smoking was more common among educated people (Ockene *et al*, 1996).

It's surprising to know that the cigarette, such a central component of our civilisation, has only been in existence for 150 years. There is little to suggest at present that it won't be around 150 years from now.

8
Opiates: heroin and the like

Any story of addiction cannot be complete without reference to this group of drugs, which have been developed from the juice of the opium poppy. Opium has been used for thousands of years, for medicine and pleasure. It was an important ingredient of the four great medicines of sixteenth century Europe: Mithridatum, Theriaca, Philonium and Disacordium.

But, its potential for misuse was well-known. Dr John James, in his *Mysteries of Opium Revealed* (1770) wrote:

> *It has been compared (not without good cause) to a permanent gentle degree of that pleasure which modesty forbids the name of.*

The heroin heroine from the movie *Trainspotting* (1996) made a similar comparison, but with a little less delicacy:

> *Better than any meat injection.*

Opiate history

The British were quick to see the vast profits that could be made from growing and selling opium. As a result we turned India into a patchwork of poppy fields, harvesting the raw opium for sale in the Far East. The emperor of China, alarmed by the stoned condition of millions of his citizens, refused to accept any further imports of opium from British India. The British decided to make a fight of it, and the result was the Opium Wars, which occurred between 1839 and 1842. The Chinese lost, and as part of the surrender terms they had to forfeit Hong Kong. It wasn't until 1997 that this highly lucrative dope deal was concluded, and Hong Kong was returned to Chinese ownership. The other British reward for victory was freedom to trade opium across China. Within 50 years millions of Chinese citizens were addicted to opium. The problem would persist until the break up of the British Empire and the 1949 communist revolution.

At the close of the nineteenth century, America was importing half a million pounds of opium each year. Although several laws governed its supply, over-the-counter opium was available in a number of potent formulations. Addiction was commonplace.

In 1908 the opium problem in the Chinese Empire prompted the creation of the Shanghai Commission, an international committee whose job it was to fight the drug menace. In response to the Commission, and partly to keep the Chinese sweet, the Americans introduced a domestic law, the Smoking Opium Act. It had little effect. Three years on the US State Department's opium commissioner, Dr Hamilton Wright declared that:

Uncle Sam is the worst drug fiend in the world.

Come to think of it, he did look hammered, and that suit was a bit of a give-away.

It was at this point that the American government made the calculation that if there were fewer drugs in the world, there would be fewer drug addicts. The result? Another convention (in the Netherlands, ironically) and the 1912 Hague Treaty, which ruled that any country growing opium or coca should drastically reduce these crops. Global drug control was to become a theme of the twentieth century.

In the nineteenth century Western man, with his fascination for fiddling with the gifts of nature, managed to produce some powerful concentrated forms of opium. Morphine was the first major derivative from raw opium, followed by the doubly strong dia-morphine or 'heroin', which was its original brand name. I expect its first manufacturer (The Bayer Company) wouldn't have believed how well it has sold over the years, and in what unusual circumstances.

There are plenty of other opiates. Codeine is a popular one, but it can't punch the same weight as heroin. Methadone is worth mentioning too. It's not strictly speaking an opiate, as it isn't made from opium, but it's chemically very similar so I'll call it an opiate to make life simpler.

Opiates are brilliant pain-killers and top drugs for taking all your troubles and dissolving them clean away. The principal problems with opiates are:

1. They're addictive.
2. They're pricey.
3. They're fairly dangerous.

The danger comes with their effect on the lungs. Opiates smother areas of the brain that control breathing, sometimes to the point where all activity drains away. Heroin has a bad reputation for this tragic event, but methadone actually claims more victims (Corkery, 1997).

Not everyone likes opiates. They can make you nauseous, give you nightmares and even bring out depression in some people. Others find them irresistible. Their appeal is down in part to everyone's friend, the brain chemical dopamine, which opiates appear to encourage. It also has a lot to do with the very relaxing sensation this group of drugs can create by occupying opiate receptor sites within the brain.

Opiate withdrawal

It takes around two to four weeks of daily use to get addicted to opiates. They are the most physically addictive of all drugs. By this I mean that when someone with an opiate habit stops taking these drugs they become quite unwell. Some people become sicker than others, but generally an addict can expect a few days of pain and discomfort of a similar intensity to a nasty bout of the flu. The major problems are muscle pains, usually in the limbs and the small of the back, sweating, vomiting, diarrhoea, and loss of sleep.

There are a few medicines around these days to help see someone through this patch, and opiate addicts may well have used them to come off their drug on more than one occasion. The fact that some addicts go back to heroin is testimony to its magnetic power, and to the almost limitless human capacity for doing the same stupid thing time and again.

In terms of shear 'addictability', heroin is only surpassed by tobacco. There's evidence that it might take up to six months for the brains of 'clean' opiate addicts to return to normal (Martin *et al*, 1973). In the meantime, they can feel abnormally low or stressed, and not be sleeping regularly, making a return to the dangerous haven of the heroin family a drawn-out temptation.

In a way heroin isn't that foreign to our bodies. We produce our own version of the stuff which, in 1975, Jerome Jaffe named 'endorphins'. The word means 'home-made morphine', and endorphins work in very similar ways to opiates. They kill pain, calm circulation and restrict our breathing. Endorphins also help fight disease, which may explain why heroin addicts often claim never to get ill, even though to the untrained eye they can look 100 per cent dreadful. Of course endorphins can also give us a warm sense of well-being. Unwitting addiction to this home-brew high is thought to be at the root of many people's obsession with going down the gym.

It can take a few weeks of daily consumption to get physically hooked to heroin. Unfortunately, once this has happened a cleaned-up former heroin addict can be back in full cramps-and-sickness withdrawal within a working week of restarting a relationship with the drug. The speed of the fall catches many former users out, trapping them again in heroin addiction, but a little deeper this next time round.

Tranquillisers: the Valium family

We all like a bit of tranquillity from time to time, and we can buy it or get it on prescription in the form of Valium.

Valium is one of a number of very similar drugs which can relax us and put us to sleep. These drugs emerged in the 1960s and were very welcome as they were infinitely less poisonous than barbiturates, the tranquillisers which had killed so many people in the mid-twentieth century (approximately 27,000 people had died using barbiturates between 1959 and 1974: Drugscope, 2000). The bad news was that they were just as addictive, despite manufacturers' claims to the contrary. Like Prozac today, doctors prescribed Valium and Librium with alarming frequency, for anything from having a job and not liking it, to not having a job and not liking it. Consequently, thousands of (mainly female) British citizens spent a miserable time towards the end of the century trying to get off these tablets.

With Valium you don't know you're hooked until you run out. In fact, because they stay in the system for a long while, you may not realise that you're addicted until two or three days after taking the last tablet. What happens next is not painful but not nice. Because tranquillisers suppress anxiety and help people to sleep, once they are gone the valium addict will experience a renewed blast of anxiety and worry, coupled with some insomnia. If someone suddenly stops taking these pills after a year or so of steady intake, there is also a danger of epileptic-type fits. Worse still, Valium withdrawal can make the user feel that they are going insane. They may begin to hallucinate, and some people have told me that they have had the impression that they were not in their own bodies, and that they were not sure precisely who they were. I'd sooner come off heroin.

Valium didn't really become a street drug until the 1980s. It was at that time that heroin addicts started to use it to stave off uncomfortable withdrawals when they'd run out of heroin. Alcoholics have also been drawn to tranquillisers, getting them from the doctor to help them to stop drinking. Some drinkers quickly found that if you take Valium and then drink, you get drunk more easily. One drinker told me that it had been a habit of his to crumble his tablets into his beer, 'To put a head on it'.

Methadone addicts have been known to use Valium to activate their methadone, making things a bit more interesting internally. From the outside it's easy to form the impression that there's not a lot going on with someone who's on a combination of opiates and Valium. This can be literally true, as post-mortems have revealed this cocktail in the blood of several dead UK citizens. Ironically, both drugs may have been prescribed by a doctor to reduce the risks of addiction.

Tranquillisers and caffeine is a very popular combination, with one American survey (Greden *et al*, 1981) finding that two-thirds of heavy coffee drinkers had reported taking a tranquilliser within the past month.

Tanquillisers are not the number one favourite drug of many people. They're more of a side dish. Like the GPs' nervous patients of a generation or two ago, most addicts and alcoholics don't realise that they are hooked on the things. They may go two or three days without any Valium, after which point it comes into their mind that they wouldn't mind buying a few tablets (the blue ones are the strongest) next time they get some heroin (which is always sooner rather than later). In this way the Valium user is unknowingly sustaining his or her addiction.

Tranquilliser addicts have a reputation for being the most severe of drug addicts (Darke, 1994). By the time they come to take these drugs they are likely to be addicted to quite a few others, and tranquillisers really put the lid on things. You can just about walk and talk on them, but you'll have little memory of either activity. Addicts like to take them (principally the sleeping tablet Temazepam) before going out shoplifting, as they give them the impression of invisibility, which is an ideal condition for law-breaking. Sounds unlikely, but a few people have reported this sensation. They're a real oblivion trip, and someone may feel comfortably in control after taking a handful of these pills, but trust me, they're not. One man I knew, a bus driver, told me that he came to his senses one day to find himself on the roof of his house, with his two young children at his side. His wife was screaming up at him from their garden, frantic with worry. He never found out how this came to happen. And no, I don't know what number bus he drives.

Opiates and alcohol: the past hundred years

Maintenance Theory (just keep taking the tablets)

In the late nineteenth century many addiction experts believed that by regularly taking a drug like morphine, the drug user's body would produce morphine antibodies, similar to the cells we naturally manufacture to trap and destroy foreign invaders like flu viruses. Without the morphine the unfortunate addict would be made sick by his own immune system. He must, therefore, have more morphine indefinitely to correct this physical imbalance. The idea was very sound but totally wrong. From it grew the tradition of drug addicts being treated by doctors. By 1919, prohibition fever had gripped America, and the idea that lovable and amusing drug addicts should still be able to get their poison while average decent folk couldn't even buy a beer didn't sit too well with most citizens. So the 40 or so clinics that had been set up across America to treat addicts with daily doses of morphine were all shut down. In the meantime, doctors were permitted to prescribe medicinal quantities of alcohol.

In Britain, the Rollerston Committee in 1926 allowed for the prescribing of opiates to morphine and heroin addicts. This practice went on into the 1960s, when methadone became the standard prescription opiate. Drug addiction at that point was still a rare thing: in the early sixties there were around 500 registered addicts in the country. Today the figure is over 50,000.

In 1929, as a response to their continuing problem, the US Government opened two 'narcotic farms' – in Kentucky and Texas – which were designed to get sick addicts off drugs and out of the penal system. The following year the Federal Bureau of Narcotics was set up to deal with the problem. Levi G Nutt, the man who was nominated to become the Bureau's first commissioner, was briskly moved aside following reports of his son making a sizable drug deal with a notorious gangster called Rothstein (Bureau of Narcotics, 1930).

Nutt's place was taken by Harry J Anslinger, a man who had made his reputation by hunting rum smugglers. Anslinger hated all drugs, and when a relatively new one (cannabis) appeared among Mexican labourers, he was very quick to realise that this 'loco-weed' had the potential to turn the mind of every decent American into that of a deranged killer. It's not clear whether Anslinger regarded dope as addictive, but that question was probably of little interest to him; he had it criminalised by 1937. If cannabis was dangerous, then heroin had to be diabolical, and in 1956 the Senate ruled that in some cases of heroin supply the death penalty could be allowed. Anslinger retired in 1962, and with him ended (at least temporarily) a no-compromise war on drugs.

Prohibition

In 1919, the Eighteenth Amendment to the American Constitution was passed, and the production and supply of alcohol was effectively banned across the United States. Only two states declined to join the ban – Rhode Island and Connecticut. And so, with high hopes for the improvement of moral, physical and economic health of the country, the era of the Prohibition began. It was to last until 1933. It's not widely known that prohibition of supply of alcohol to Native Americans began a hundred years earlier, and persisted until 1953. Many Native American tribes are voluntarily abstinent today.

Alcohol prohibition was ended because, despite a massive police effort, it couldn't work. There were some gains in terms of public health, but some dreadful losses. The worst of these was probably the forgotten tragedy of a liquid tonic made from the extract of Jamaican ginger. It also contained a large proportion of alcohol. To get round the prohibition laws it was registered as a medicine and sold in drug stores (chemists). As it was barely legal, production standards were poor, and a dangerous chemical called TCP leaked into the finished product. As a consequence 50,000 Americans were permanently paralysed (Morgan, 1982).

Similar tragedies happen today with adulterated heroin, and one may be left to wonder exactly who is truly protected by the prohibition laws. The black market and organised crime is one of the most efficient means of commercial distribution. It uses modern sophisticated marketing techniques alongside the older proven methods of bribery and intimidation. In times of war this system can deliver products that entire armed forces can't provide. It shouldn't surprise us therefore that the war against drugs appears lost.

One solution would appear to be licensed legalisation, where governments sell limited quantities of clean drugs at a price that undercuts organised crime (Marks, 1996). This is a similar method to the Norwegian alcohol policy, which has resulted in that country having the healthiest livers in Europe. It won't stop addiction, but it may just reduce it – something that the current Western system has failed to do. The illegality of a drug appears to have little bearing on a citizen's decision to take it (Wilkens *et al*, 1997), and the legalisation of a substance (as in the case of strong beer in Iceland, for example, [Olafsdottir, 1997]) does not appear to cause epidemic use. And drug seizures have been found to result in no change to price availability or purity (Weatherburn and Lind, 1997).

The sixties and onward

LSD, interesting though it is, doesn't impact greatly on the story of modern addiction. Picking up mundane household objects such as a potato peeler or box of cornflakes and studying them with daft wonder for half the night doesn't impress anyone who hasn't got a decade to waste. The fact is that as an experience, LSD is so unpredictable, tiring, profound and unsettling that no one but a dedicated masochist would make it part of his daily routine.

The influence LSD has had on addiction is to allow people to think of drugs as mind-expanding, forging a new awareness, integrating parts of the psyche which had been previously unknown to the majority of Western society, radically altering the way we think of ourselves and of each other. True of LSD, but not true of Brown Ale. So the drug explosion of the sixties was partly fuelled by the mistaken idea that drugs enriched the mind, rather than shaking the poor thing around a fair bit or slowly frying it.

People were beginning to take drugs in increasing numbers, and the old 'Reefer Madness' propaganda of the Anslinger days became the source of hilarity. Popular culture began to support drug-taking: movies like *Easy Rider* and performers such as Bob Dylan and The Doors openly encouraged the use of chemicals. In astute desperation President Nixon appointed Elvis Presley Special Drug Enforcer. The King posed for the cameras shaking Nixon's hand, looking moderately vague as several powerful opiates and sedatives cruised through his regal nervous system. The game was up – America was out to lunch.

By the 1980s a greater drug problem than heroin blighted America. Cocaine use had increased rapidly in the preceding decade, and it's associations with glamour, money and sex made it the ideal drug of the day. Billions of US dollars drained from the American economy into the cartels of Central and South America. Just as things appeared to have reached their worst, a new more potent form of the drug appeared. Crack is a smokable crystallised lump of cocaine, very quick-acting, very elevating and very persuasive. It's use became endemic in deprived urban areas, and the big money to be made from it, coupled with crack's capacity to make users paranoid and highly reactive, has led to some severe incidents of violence (Dawson, 1998).

Methadone

Methadone had been a street drug in the mid-twentieth century. It's nickname was 'dolly', after its trade name of Dolphine. Methadone was brought into drug treatment in the 1960s as a means of keeping addicts from injecting street drugs, which are often far from sanitary. A daily 'dose' of methadone, usually in the form of a drinkable linctus is prescribed by the doctor as a substitute for heroin, keeping withdrawals at bay.

Being on methadone alone is quite boring, and drug addicts don't take drugs with the intention of getting bored. Taking other drugs 'on top' of methadone is often not viable, as these may be detected by urine testing, and the methadone prescription stopped as a result. Alcohol is a legitimate alternative. It may not be exotic, but it's better than nothing. Nothing is an extremely depressing amount to a dedicated addict. Approximately a quarter of addicts on methadone programmes have been found to be suffering from alcoholism (Bickel *et al*, 1987; Joseph and Appel, 1985).

The main reason for giving methadone to opiate addicts is the greater good of the public. There's evidence that methadone programmes have helped to contain the spread of HIV across the European Community (Farrell, 1995). It seems that crime is also reduced by the supply of this drug to drug addicts (Farrell *et al*, 1994). A massive American survey calculated that for every dollar spent on giving methadone to heroin addicts, four dollars was saved by the US judicial system and insurance companies (Harwood *et al*, 1988). Treatment as a whole (abstinence as well as methadone prescription) was recently estimated to bring about a £3 saving for every pound spent (NTORS, 1999).

Methadone has also been given to coke addicts with moderate success (Magura *et al*, 1991). Once again, it can hardly be surprising that people don't take so much of one drug if they're given plenty of another.

In the absence of a better idea, and for sound pragmatic reasons, methadone remains the most common treatment for opiate addiction among many wealthier nations.

9
The sex addict

Some people believe that they are addicted to sex. 'Sex addict'? Doesn't that just mean 'Got caught'? When it comes to us blokes, we're all sex addicts really – we just happen to spend large periods of our lives in enforced abstinence. Let's face facts: we are biologically pre-programmed to keep the species from extinction. This is why we think about sex every two minutes. Sounds like we're stuck in some terrible thought loop. Not a bit of it – until the invention of the motorcar and the electric drill, our minds were a blank for the remaining 90 seconds. There remains, however, a fair gap between just thinking about something and actually doing it, and the sex addict is someone who is more doing than thinking.

If it's just a question of being hooked on the sensation of orgasm, does the sex addict really need anyone else around? One or two men have told me that they have had episodes of binge masturbating. This might involve locking themselves away for a couple of days or more and engaging in serial self-abuse. To spice things up a bit there's probably a stack of porn to hand, and sometimes items of women's underwear, to at least give the bloke the impression that his mental movies feature some romantic interest.

The solitary approach to sexual ecstasy may suit some of our citizens, but for the majority of us sex is really a shared endeavour. Another body is required. Some sex addicts will satisfy themselves by using prostitutes, or clocking up crippling bills on telephone sex lines. Others will go out in search of other sex addicts, with a wild time in mind. Sex addicts, in their need for mutual satisfaction, have an uncanny ability to recognise one another. On first meeting, eye contact is sustained for a moment or two beyond the unspoken cultural limit. When we offer our gaze to a stranger, we signal some intention: hostility, warmth, curiosity. The sex-addict's eyes read invitation and challenge. Secret knowledge is exchanged, and conversation is secondary as the game of seduction and counter-seduction begins.

The purpose of the game is principally sexual burglary. Break in, take what you can, and leave without attracting the attention of the authorities. Both players look to escape without personal injury, so the lust game is a bizarre contradiction of physical intimacy and emotional distance. Sex addicts don't need to like each other to play, as sex for its own sake is a competitive game. Your partner is, in a sense, your opponent; if you dislike them, so much the better. The stakes are then raised – should you fail to reach your opponent's expectations, humiliation awaits. If your athleticism and imagination prove supreme, the glow of victory is yours, and with it, the right to pass a withering remark as you close the door behind you.

It may be artificial to divide sex addicts between male and female teams. Sex addiction is fundamentally a solo sport, and every one – regardless of gender – has a unique internal world. That said, the female sex addict may operate under a different set of motivations and risks to the male. As far as she's concerned, there are plenty of people out there she wouldn't touch with a barge pole.

We men have standards too, but ours tend to be conspicuously lower. Once the female addict has seen the man to whom she's attracted, (we'll assume she's heterosexual), she can be very thorough in the arrangement of his seduction. Clothing, appearance, location and 'chance' meetings are all pre-planned. The female addict may have yet to make any contact with her prey, but she is now firmly in the addictive loop. Her thoughts are dominated by this man, and the fantasy of how he is: strong, affectionate, clever, rich, and capable of bringing her a life of unrelenting joy. While all this is going on, real life recedes into the background. There's no need to fret about anything, because any day now everything is going to be perfect.

The big night finally arrives, and – at last – the female love/sex addict finds herself in the embrace of her dream man: a perfect blend of George Clooney and St Francis of Assissi. It may take only moments of being alone together for it to dawn on her that in reality he's a 24-carat pratt.

Worse still, he could actually be an alarming combination of Grant Mitchell and the Marquis de Sade. Rather than lying in the arms of a naïve and kindly Adonis-next-door, the female sex addict may find that she is in the company of a male sex addict. The feigned innocence of her own approach work had been met at every turn by an equally false response from Mr Wonderful. Now she is naked, alone, and next to a stronger male who doesn't care at all about her, but is deeply interested in all kinds of functions her body might be manoeuvred into serving. You said you were good. You said you were up for anything. You want to play, so let's play. Degradation beckons.

Sex addicts don't generally pair up for long. All that domesticity is a bit of a passion-killer, and intimacy is of limited interest to a sex addict. They are tapped into something far more powerful – the forbidden fire. The sex addict may settle down with their partner, a tolerant sort, chosen with the prospect of infidelity in mind. The partner will have to be forgiving, because – as a vampire needs fresh blood – the sex addict must have new flesh. In fact, the appeal of Count Dracula may be down to the fact that he's a meta-phorical sex addict. All those virgins and beds and succulent necks.

But Dracula came unstuck, and so too does the sex addict. It's an occupational hazard. When they are found out, everyone wants them punished. They've been getting away with the one thing we're not allowed to do, and envy soon turns to judgement. 'I don't know why she puts up with him', 'He's had nothing but trouble with her'. Tears are shed, crockery is smashed, and final warnings are issued. She often does 'put up with him' though. There are few partners who are more attentive and considerate than the husband who's just been caught cheating. A strange kind of revenge is exacted, with the wronged partner making the guilty spouse pay for their misadventures. He'll stay in, buy flowers, not argue back, and finally decorate the spare room.

For a while the home is a domestic haven, with the couple pulling together to put the past behind them. But the pre-occupation with wild sex drives on, the passions climb, and (sooner or later) opportunity and impulse coincide. Eventually the destructive power of addiction can't be endured, and the repeated cycle of affairs cause the marriage to end. Alternatively, there's an unspoken agreement between the partners. As long as he's being discrete he can carry on. The pay off for her may be that she holds the power to bring him to book at any time. But let's get back to the fun.

The sex addict has a single purpose – an intense experience. He or she knows what they like, so they set about getting it. The sex becomes quite ritualised and complicated: various devices, bizarre outfits, visual media may all have to be incorporated. The bedroom's so full there's nowhere to put your slippers. And no room for emotion or spontaneity either. The sex addict must be in control. Nothing must spoil the attainment of ecstasy. Absolute control guarantees absolute satisfaction.

There are a couple or three ideas around as to what makes a sex addict. Sex is the simplest of all. The sex addict is good at it and just loves it. People don't necessarily wonder what drives someone to spend a large proportion of their lives sat by the side of a lake, trying to catch a fish. We're all satisfied that they love fishing. Which do you prefer?

Maybe sex addicts have more sex hormones than the average

person, making them just plain horny. Or perhaps it's all psychological again, with the male looking to take revenge on his neglectful mother, via a succession of women, all of whom he'll misuse; the female sex addict could be unconsciously attempting to attract the care and attentions of a stern or remote father. If Patrick Carnes' figures are correct (Carnes, 1991), eight out of ten sex addicts are the victims of sexual abuse, and 97% of sex addicts interviewed reported that their childhoods had been emotionally abusive. These experiences can leave the survivor with combined difficulties in the areas of sex, love and relationships. Deep down, the sex addict may believe that no-one could love them for who they truly are, so he or she may as well grab sex/love by being who they truly are not. This false self can be a considerable drag, as it's he or she (the false self) that gets all the attention through playing an outdated game of doctors and nurses, leaving the true self feeling empty and neglected. This empty true self is an experience which is common to all addictions.

Sex is a powerful thing. European history is filled with examples of peace being made between nations through the exchange of sex, ie. the marriage of one nation's Princess to a rival King. Contractual sex (marriage) remains the foundation of many of our world's societies. Something so powerful is bound to prove irresistible to a number of us. Plus, the experience of having the complete physical surrender of another person can't fail but to make you feel anything but special: maybe it's this feeling that is so addictive. Who wants to feel ordinary?

> *I'm special,*
> *So special*
> *I've got to have some of your attention,*
> *Give it to me!*

> Chrissie Hynde, *Brass in Pocket*, 1978

Sex, drink and drugs

Why have one when you can have it all? This is a question that appeals to the logic of addiction. Some drugs make sex impossible. Heroin lowers libido, and too much alcohol can lead to the infamous brewer's droop. But a moderate amount of drink, and dope too, are widely regarded as aphrodisiacs. As their names suggest, the stimulant drugs (eg. amphetamine and coke) have the capacity to enhance sex. That said, we're all built differently, and I have met people who enjoy a full sex-life as heroin addicts, and I know others who have no sexual appetite when under the influence of speed or coke.

Many enthusiasts of uppers use them for the purpose of improved or prolonged sex. They do better with the drug than without. In fact, if they don't have the drug, this type of addict wouldn't know where to start. Many addicts have been using drugs on a highly regular basis since adolescence. Consequently, they've never made love without chemical assistance/alteration. Straight sex can be a scary prospect, a second virginity.

If there is a number one sex/pleasure drug around at the moment, it has to be crack. The orgasmic rush and sensation of invulnerability that are characteristic of the drug mirrors the experience of sex very closely. The exchange of (often oral) sex for money, or simply for crack itself, is a common feature of the crack lifestyle. The sexually impulsive nature of coke in either form (powder or crystal) is a major influence in the spread of HIV.

Alcohol is the most widely used drug of seduction. Drink's ability to reduce the flow of thoughts that normally tell us that something may not be such a great idea after all, means that regrettable choices can be made under its influence. Men and women have claimed that they feel more sexy after a drink (Wilsnack, 1980), but alcohol actually suppresses female sexual arousal, so the anticipation is usually better than the event.

10
Food

The purpose of this chapter is not to look in depth at the nature of problem eating. This would be beyond the scope of my knowledge and experience. Instead, I'll try to identify areas where eating and addiction overlap.

As we've already seen (see *Chapter 3, p.32–36*) eating food is something our nervous system tells us that we should do on a regular basis. Food is one of life's joys, and many of us have to be careful not to over-indulge in the pleasure of eating for fear of being identified as a 'fat greedy pig'.

One group of people in our society who don't have much difficulty in limiting what they eat are people who suffer from depression. When you're seriously down it's difficult to extract pleasure from anything the world has to offer. It is significantly common for people suffering from depression to have the same lack of appetite for food itself (Strober and Katz, 1990). Eating can be a dismal experience.

Alternatively, food can be way too attractive to other citizens. They consistently overeat, either ballooning to the dimensions of a modest airship, or keeping the fat at bay by making themselves vomit or by purging with laxatives. Others may eat voraciously and starve in turns, unable to escape from this vicious circle.

What unites all these food problems is the domination that eating has over the thoughts and actions of sufferers. To go further, it seems that all eating problems are a means to distancing people from some inner unhappiness. You can't be unhappy when you're preoccupied – there isn't the time. Equally, you can't feel happy as the obsession keeps you in a pair of emotional blinkers. The idea is that to a person with an eating problem food means more than simply food: it has some deep-seated emotional importance. This may explain why it's ultimately impossible for a binge-eater to avoid the next gorging orgy. It's not just peckishness going on – all kinds of unease are beginning to surface and must therefore be kept in. Swallowed.

It was Melanie Klein who wrote about just how traumatic hunger could be to us all as babies (it's quite upsetting to write this, so skip to the next paragraph if you like). Our cry would be so loud and so piercing that we'd wake our mother from the deepest sleep. Klein wondered though what might happen to the hungry child who could not wake his or her mother. Perhaps they weren't there, or were so out of it they were dead to the world (interesting phrase). The child would then experience a terrible panic and this panic would be locked into the developing little one's mind. Panic equals hunger. Dread equals hunger. Decades later this grown-up child is having a bad day. Things are going wrong in the home or at work. They feel out of control and things are crowding in on her or him. The overriding thought that comes into the mind is food. Panic isn't experienced, but a gnawing kind of hunger is. The result is binge eating or perhaps starvation. So, if Klein was right, eating problems can go back to the cot.

I remember talking with Kerry, a female drug addict, who told me that the one addiction she hated the most was to chocolate. Kerry described how she would sit at home and try to resist opening a bottle of wine. If she cracked and had a glass or two she might then find herself smoking the heroin she'd promised herself not to touch. But last of all, and with the deepest feelings of regret and shame, Kerry went for the family-size bar of Fruit and Nut. Now I don't know whether Cadbury's would be interested in an advertising campaign that claims their product is harder to resist than heroin, but Kerry's experience is a measure of how big a problem eating can be to the sufferer.

Some people with eating disorders have an encyclopaedic knowledge of the calorific value of different foods. If you were to ask them how many calories does a digestive biscuit have, they may immediately respond, 'Which brand?' It's not uncommon for binge eaters to keep drawers and even wardrobes packed with secret stashes of their objects of obsession and desire, particularly the hard-core merchandise – chocolates, cakes, biscuits, etc.

Once control has been lost and the temptation to gorge on all these goodies has proved too much, some of the patterns found in chemical addiction begin to emerge. The loss of control can be extreme, with bingers using both hands to satisfy the feeding frenzy. Next comes the 'rush', as highly combustible refined sugar courses round the blood stream. At this point the binger may 'bale-out', and force her/himself to be sick, or they may keep the food on board. Energy has then to be diverted to the digestive system, causing a kind of dopiness to settle in the binger's brain. This is an exaggerated form of the torpid, sleepy feeling we get when we doze in front of some dated old movie after a heavy Sunday dinner. Our over-eating friend has now reached a point of oblivion, which may have been his or her original destination: food has been used as an anaesthetic, to numb the body and the mind. If you have no real sense of your body and mind, you have nothing. Nothing means no thoughts and no difficult emotions. Everything vanishes in a warm deadening fog.

As the mist clears regrets may soon follow, and the self-denial stage begins. The binge eater may next starve her or himself, and make heartfelt pledges not to lose control again. This too has echoes of chemical dependence, where binge coke users or drinkers attempt to get things back on track by keeping off their poison for a while. It may also relate to the way addicts sometimes have of disregarding or denying what they need emotionally. Don't worry about me – I'm fine. An anorexic teenager is often described by her family as a lovely girl, who never gave us any trouble, a bit quiet perhaps… It's sometimes said of an alcoholic that he's a lovely fella when he's not on the drink. So nice it isn't true…

Now there may be very different reasons for these similar observations. The alcoholic may have good reason to be a model of virtuous behaviour when he's not drinking. He may simply have put the horns away and be sporting the halo for a while. With the anorexic something very different may be happening, something to do with their actual concrete physical self as well as their social self.

This idea goes back to the story of Tanya (see *Chapter 1, p.10*). Basically, we have to learn where we begin and where we end. The correct answer, of course, is at the top of our heads and the bottom of our feet. Simple. But not everyone figures this out. People suffering from autism, for instance, can find it very hard to work out where they end and everything else begins. It's possible that anorexics have a similar difficulty in getting a fixed idea, a definition, of their bodies. Things get a bit blurred. They therefore have to guess at their body's form or shape. The idea is quite neat, but it doesn't quite answer the question, 'Why then does every anorexic person think that they're fat? Where are the people who guess in the opposite direction, and believe that they're too thin?'

There are loads of theories as to what is wrong with anorexics, ranging from, 'They have a very funny virus', to 'They're mad'. The idea that fits best with addiction is two-fold:

- First, there's the brain chemistry pay-off. Moses led his people into the desert and they didn't eat for 40 days and 40 nights. They were starving. They began to enter a rarefied level of consciousness, seeing visions of God. In other words, not eating is mind-altering. Saints and mystics throughout the ages have denied themselves food as a method to attaining this sense of the divine. Anorexics may therefore have stumbled on this very economic way to lift their spirits.

- Second, power is very intoxicating. We talk about others (never ourselves) being drunk on power, or of a job promotion going straight to someone's head. Anorexia gives the sufferer the power to self-destruct. The result is very similar to that in the case of alcoholism or drug addiction (see *Chapter 8*), namely that everyone around this pitifully thin person is mesmerised by fear for what might happen next. Not eating is a tremendously powerful statement about how you feel about your world. The protestors Bobby Sands and Mahatma Ghandi used this simple act of refusing food to draw attention to their cause. Only one of them survived. As a species we find self-starvation causes incredible turmoil within us. It's dangerous and unnatural. Relatives of someone suffering from anorexia experience all kinds of uncomfortable feelings in the presence of this horrible affliction. Helplessness, fear, anger and shame are perhaps the four most common emotions felt by the sufferer's family.

Helplessness: One of our primary instincts is to nurture our offspring, and an inability to do this can cause awful distress. Family members will therefore try everything within their power to get their loved one to eat. The anorexic is too strong to be bullied, charmed or tricked from their path. Finally it becomes all too clear that nothing is going to work. The illness has the family trapped; yet the sufferer can't see the problem at all. Here, anorexia differs from chemical addictions, in that the drinkers or drug addicts can experience moments of insight that show them just how big a jam they're really in. At these instants, the chemical addict feels the full impact of helplessness. In anorexia, by contrast, insight is a thousand miles away. While to the rest of the world they may look like a skull on a stick, the person with anorexia believes herself or himself to be definitely not too thin. If anything, they're still a bit overweight. Their condition is almost helpless, but they just don't see it. Their addiction to the power that starvation gives them should bring about feelings of helplessness – let's face it, death is stalking them – but they feel fine. The truth is that with such a tragedy relentlessly unfolding in the core of a family home, somebody has got to not feel fine. So the helplessness of addiction is passed to the relatives without the sick loved one even realising it.

Fear: In a way, by declining food, someone is denying life itself. They've got no appetite for it. The person with the food problem may have a fear of not fitting in, fear of failing, or a fear of anything and everything. But all that comes into their awareness is the necessity to eat or not to eat. Again this may be the unconscious mind working, hiding all this fear and anxiety about ourselves and our lives, and converting it into stuff about our diet and our bodies. Julia Buckroyd (1996) puts this idea quite clearly when she says that in the mind of the over- or non-eater, emotional troubles are translated into something that can't be understood by the outsider. What we get is fearful on the part of our ill friend or relation. They stay strangely serene, as they are either starving their emotions by refusing to feed them, or suffocating them by piling food on top.

Anger: As already suggested, there seems to be a connection between difficulties with eating normally, and the capacity to show our feelings. The stereotypical anorexic, for instance, tends to be passive, apparently free of any strong opinions or emotions. She's not the sort of person to start a street brawl. In fact, she's probably unlikely to stand out in a crowd. This may be why she shrinks herself to the dimensions of a shadow. She's looking to be overlooked. But being passed over, or met with a blend of disgust and pity, can be extremely hurtful. Once again, addiction has the remedy to such painful experiences: don't experience them. Instead, go home as soon as possible and submerge yourself in such nutrition-related activities as eating a pyramid of pies, or taking a fistful of laxatives, or engaging in a mad session of exercise. The humiliating events of a few hours earlier are soon lost in the thrall of the calorie war.

Because it is a war of sorts, Susie Orbach (1998) has pointed out, problem eating features some very angry acts – biting, tearing, stuffing, chewing, purging, vomiting. A favourite military strategy has long been the besieging and starving-out of the enemy. At times this is the sort of treatment someone with an eating problem hands out to her or his own body. Their anger may be justified but it's misdirected. It's as if they've got mad with the wrong person. As Carla Wills-Brandon (1995) points out, with compulsive eating or starving, food is not the enemy; the sufferer's body is the enemy. She or he will ruthlessly scan their anatomy for the slightest indication of stored fat. Once identified, the offending mass must be eliminated by means of a systematic campaign.

Shame: Shame of our physical selves goes back a long way. In a historical sense it goes back to our first ancestors Adam and Eve getting caught with their trousers down:

> *Then the eyes of both of them were opened, and they realised that they were naked.*

Genesis 3.7

Original sin, the biblical idea that our bodies are a kind of crime, may still have some influence over us. We tend to keep our clothes on in public, and we've built up a complex system of sex laws. Personal shame can start at the point where we struggle to become potty trained, or when we make startling sexual discoveries of ourselves. So, whether it's a matter of wetting ourselves, or drifting into sexual exploration, our bodies can make it possible for us to do the forbidden. In short, our bodies, fantastically useful that they are, can bring us into conflict with the rules. By keeping to the rules, standards and expectations of our community, we can be accepted. Failure to comply with these codes invites the application of the number one instrument of social control, shame. Parents, teachers, other children, the old woman down the street, disapproval rains down on us from every quarter during our childhood, knocking us into shape. Shame burns like hell, so to avoid it we simply and absolutely must fit in.

The dread of not fitting in may get translated literally by some into the thought that they are the wrong shape piece to find a place in the mosaic of society. Too fat, in their words. They may just be deluded, or they could be seeing things as they really stand, namely that large people are, for reasons that are mainly beyond me, unacceptable. They paid for the food, didn't they? And where's the fat one in *Friends*? Some people are just bigger than others, anyway.

Back to the point. In the case of someone who really isn't overweight but believes themselves to be, the cause of the misconception can only be guessed at. If the root of it is in the emotion of shame, perhaps he or she has been made to feel that way by the cruelty or neglect of others, or by the violation of his or her body through sexual abuse – something that is common in sex addiction. To fit in there's always the option of weight control through extreme tactics. You then no longer have the shame of being too large. Rather, you have the secret shame of what you've been up to to keep the weight off. With bulimia the sufferer may throw others off the scent by cooking delicious meals for everyone, and publicly eating no more than the next person. Perhaps to ease feelings of guilt and shame, a binge eater will often tempt others to eat, and may spend a large proportion of her or his time in the kitchen, close to the source of their obsession.

Someone who suffers from bulimia (and again this is a criminal generalisation), tends to present a highly acceptable face to the world. They are cheerful, caring and capable. Their appearance (clothes, hair, make-up) is often immaculate, because with bulimia appearance is crucial. Just below the surface lies the desperation of eating and purging mayhem. Bulimia is perhaps the most isolating of all the food addictions in that no-one can see you have it. Like the binge drinker, the bulimia sufferer has time to come up for air and experience remorse for losing control, but unlike the alcoholic, nobody can really tell what's gone on. There are no tell-tale empty bottles or stale alcohol odours. The one clue can be a sound of retching from behind the bathroom door. This is the singular thing that the highly capable, well-put-together binge eater may not be able to conceal.

With an eating problem, shame is held inside the self, and the body may therefore be regarded as a traitor, a guilty partner. The body must be diminished, or concealed in baggy shapeless clothing, or de-sexed through starvation, so that the breast and hips shrink. In sexual addiction, by contrast, tight-fitting and revealing clothes are used to enhance sexy bumps and curves. The sex addict can't feel shame because he or she is shameless. They believe that unrestrained sexual activity was their idea in the first place, and they are therefore totally free, rather than a puppet to what happened years before.

11
Addiction and the family

It's very common for drug addicts to have had ancestors who were alcoholics. Miller *et al* (1990), for instance, said that over 50% of male and 62% of female cocaine addicts they had studied in 1990 had a family history of alcoholism. Obviously, if as a child you see vital role models frequently worse for wear, you may take on a fundamental lesson about life and chemicals, namely that it's OK to be a responsible adult and to get out of it. Yu and Perrine (1997) interviewed drunk drivers about their family background, and found that a father's drinking tended to have more influence on the son, while a daughter's drinking habits were more likely to be copied from her mother. To an extent, the drug you choose is immaterial, although older relatives may have pretty strong views about exactly how acceptable cocaine is in contrast to, say, brandy.

The influence may go back further than a conscious memory of mum or dad getting drunk. As an infant, a child of an alcoholic might well have been taken into parties and pubs where he or she would be exposed to the sounds and smells of drinking. To be lifted from the cot and cuddled and kissed by an adult with alcohol on their breath is to have a potentially lifelong mental link established from the very first weeks of life. This connection between drink and care may be all the stronger for happening so early in a child's development, at a time when no words exist, or at least the understanding of words. Before we have language we are totally reliant on our senses for working out what is going on. In the infant world, cuddles plus soothing sounds plus the smell of cheap sherry equals love.

This simplistic idea can't truly explain addiction, but it may have an influence (Fossey, 1993). It's impossible to say, as we have so many formative experiences in the first couple of years of life, which we can never recall. But they're in there somewhere, contributing a piece toward the jigsaw of our personalities.

Naturally the influence of our childhood experiences doesn't stop once we learn to talk. When we do get language into our bones we become conscious little people. We have words for things that happen around us, and words help us to form memories. We remember parties, rows, laughter, bottles and the telly, Sundays at gran's house, our first day at school, days out with auntie and uncle, and a holiday in the Canaries. In short, childhood.

Each family has its own unique set of rules that are far from being a miniature replication of society's rules and values. Once inside the family home the outside laws no longer automatically apply. We are now in another realm – the kingdom of the dominant adult.

We accept everything that happens to us as children as normal. I've known incredibly brave people who have survived the most brutal upbringing featuring a violent dad, a beaten, drunken mum and a rapist step-dad. When I've asked them how they ever kept from going under they've often said, 'I thought it was normal. I didn't know any different'. To go one step further, everything that doesn't happen in our childhood is abnormal to us. If most of our family drink, family life without drink is abnormal. If most of our family mistreat us, family life where we don't get mistreated is abnormal.

Life experiences are like a map for us. When we leave childhood and go our own way we use this map to find our way around the big bad world. We don't generally go to places off the map. We click with people whose ways we understand. We can predict what they're going to say or do next, which is reassuring. We might predict that by midnight they're going to be drunk and argumentative. Sounds like a problem, but we've dealt with hundreds of scenes like these so far in life, so among all this drunken nonsense we're really quite relaxed: in control, even.

And it's not just about the people we meet, this map of our world. It's about the things we do as well: it's our birthday; it's Saturday night, let's go to the pub then on to a nightclub; it's Sunday afternoon, let's get a bottle of wine and settle down in front of the television. We're creatures of habit, and a number of these habits we pick up in childhood. We follow the rituals of our families, what we eat, what we say, where we go, what we do when we get there. From this point of view it's not hard to see how a son or daughter of a family who drink heavily, or use more drugs than enough, go on to follow suit.

Things can be very different in the case of the hopeless drunk or drug addict in a family of moderate and responsible individuals. This black sheep is an almost constant source of worry and irritation to his or her sober relatives. The family spin in a helpless orbit round the sick relative, caught up in the emotions that loving someone so clearly not right can evoke. Come down too hard on the alcoholic and he may get worse, placate him and he may get worse, do nothing and he may get worse. Beyond the drinking, there's often the additional fear of how unpredictable the reactions of an alcoholic might be. It can be like tiptoeing across a minefield, with the risk of a sudden explosion never far from the long-suffering relative's mind.

What has happened is that addiction has given the sufferer power as well as weakness. Someone may be unable to function without one or several chemicals, or to sustain a relationship or hold down a job, but within the home this effectively handicapped person is central to what can happen in the lives of everyone in that building. The power may have come from the addict daring to set himself against the unwritten laws of the family, not just in the compulsive use of chemicals but also in a challenging stance against family values. The 'druggie' son may sometimes be consciously or unconsciously rebelling against emotional sterility, for instance. That's not to say that if he then goes on to become a drug addict and remains so at 30 years old, he is still taking drugs to upset his father. As Alex Georgakis (2000) points out, the reason why someone started to take a drug is rarely the reason why they take it several years later. Most middle-aged nicotine addicts don't light up to look cool or shock their elders. But it's equally true that the need to feel more important or complete or powerful puts some future addicts on the first step of the ladder to total disaster.

It's even worth considering that a 30-year-old drug addict is still rebelling against the family, society, or our solar system for that matter. It has long been a popular idea among addiction 'experts' that the addict is emotionally immature (Kraepelin, 1883). The thought is that personal development gets frozen at the point at which the addict begins to get stuck into the drink or the drugs. New experiences that help adjust and refine the way most of us react to the world around us don't generally happen to the addict. He's too busy repeating old experiences in the Red Lion or at his mate's flat. It's strangely reassuring to find someone who seems to be making even more of a mess of his/her life than we are, but whether it's fair to kick him/her when they're down is doubtful. Certainly, many addicts have a childlike quality to them, but this is engaging rather than pathetic. The stereotype of the immature addict disintegrates when you meet a successful businessperson or a dedicated social worker who has become ensnared by addiction.

But addiction is about dependence. Dependence on a drug, or dependence on an activity that delivers its own brand of thrill, such as sex or gambling. As the dependence deepens, the addict becomes increasingly unreliable and bad at keeping things together. Dependence on things then demands dependence on other people. People who used to be productive become dependent on state benefits; people who used to be independent can go backwards and lean on their families. I've met numerous addicts and alcoholics who have returned to the home of their ageing parents years after they left. In a survey of 100 American drug addicts, Vaillant (1966) found that virtually every one of the 30 who became drug-free were living independently of their parents. Rather than suffering from emotional immaturity, it's possible that many addicts were as mature as their contemporaries until addiction took hold, causing a sort of emotional regression or de-maturing (not that there is such a word). This idea is also not new (Cutten, 1908).

There have been efforts over the years to discover whether a particular style of parenting can cause a range of psychological problems (Bateson, 1956). In the case of addiction, studies have suggested that a kind of smothering or over-invasive family atmosphere makes it more likely that a child will develop an addiction problem (Kaufman, 1976). The idea here is that an over-involved mother can do all the thinking, feeling and acting for the child. They are stuck under her wing, protected from the harsh winds of the adult world. Any time things go wrong the son looks for something outside of himself to make things feel better. It used to be mum; it ends up being a gramme of heroin or eight cans of Carlsberg Special Brew. Still, the bond between son and mother (or daughter and father for that matter) remains airtight. They will protect them from angry drug debtors, from the police, and (with far less success) from themselves. This type of good-intentioned but suffocating parent will do absolutely anything for their child with the exception of the one thing that might really help – letting them go.

The son or daughter's 'problem' now becomes the whole story as far as mum and dad are concerned. Any ill health suffered is blamed on the errant child, but the parents can't or won't let the young addict go. Their attempts to shame them into giving up ('Can't you see what you're doing to your mother? And my heart murmur won't take much more of this') only make their son's habit worse, as he struggles with the dual burden of coping with a growing addiction and the responsibility of the physical and mental well-being of the entire family. The family then get angrier and more interfering, in the mistaken belief that this will work in the end.

According to this way of looking at family life (Minuchin, 1975), the addict son or daughter is enacting a disharmony in the family that may have existed before they were even born. They can't answer the parents' question, 'Why can't you stop?', because they don't know why they started. It's all unconscious. The uneasy vibes in the home have been accumulated by the addict-to-be. He feels awkward and sort of tense and unhappy, but he doesn't know why. One day he takes a drug and wham! Suddenly he feels alright. It's as if the rest of his experience has been in some way wrong, and this chemical experience is right. He resolves to take drugs on a regular basis.

Meanwhile, the family still does not have a natural and relaxed way of being together. It's unhealthy, but it's a lot more convenient for almost every member if someone else takes the blame and becomes 'the sick one'. Then everyone can be shocked and dismayed and angry and totally without blame. It's an odd paradox – the person who is clearly being the most irresponsible, namely the out-of-control addict son, is the most responsible member of the family. He admits his fault. He is a junky, fair enough. He'll even take the blame for all the unhappiness in the rest of the home. Meanwhile the family can remain glued together by its own sickness, which is a dreadful state of affairs, but just about preferable to the whole thing falling apart and each member being exposed to the realities of how they really feel about themselves and each other.

Don't get me wrong, the lad's no angel or martyr. He gets the obvious reward of the drugs, and possibly some secret pleasure from seeing everyone so concerned and stressed out. And he'll never admit to pawning his mother's engagement ring, even though it was he who did it. It's going to take a bunch of counsellors a month of Sundays to sort this one out.

There's no average family, and lumping families together into categories is of very limited value, but if you've got three minutes to spare, let's do it anyway.

The first family that might nurture addiction is the crisis family. The crisis family has things going wrong on a very regular basis, and all kinds of people are drawn in to help its adult members sort out the chaos – doctors, social workers, the children. The crisis family is spectacularly irresponsible but likeable with it. The parents show the next generation that it's OK to be inconsistent, and not to cope. No-one can escape because they get called at all hours of the day and night. Life's never dull with the crisis family – fights, laughs, divorce and (of course) plenty of drugs all go to make up a crazy house.

The second family is the clan. With the clan the message is drummed in from childhood – it's a hostile world so we've got to stick together. The clan must be tough and prepared to back one another up in a row. Loyalty is everything, and the more aggressive and harsh you can be toward outsiders, the more love you show to the family. Not that love gets a mention. In fact any emotion other than anger is out of bounds. As an addiction specialist I would strongly recommend you not to take a clan member's parking space. Although it must always join forces against anyone else, the clan can fight among itself. I knew one clan where the father's last words to his sons were 'I'm going to knock you out'. They were busily engaged in a fight at the side of the old fellow's deathbed. The clan are out of their heads quite a lot of the time; the most comfortable place to be when you have to survive in a set-up like this.

The final family is the regimented family. Things are very rigid in this house, with little talk and loads of rules. Praise is limited and the overall message is: you don't quite measure up. Mistakes are not allowed – they're seen as examples of slackness or selfish thinking. The regimental parent believes that disaster is never far away, so constant vigilance and absolute effort are essential. There's just about no drinking, and certainly no drug-taking permitted in the regimented family. All rebellion goes on under the surface. In a regimented family it's hard to tell who's up to what.

Common sense also says that a loose 'do-your-own-thing' style of parenting isn't going to offer tremendous protection from drug misuse. Poor adult supervision has been found to be a factor in the development of some addiction (Crundall, 1993). Freedom to make our own mistakes can assist independence (and independence is, of course, the opposite of dependence), so perhaps a moderately liberal style of parenting could make addiction less likely as opposed to more so.

Relationships

The main reason why adult females become addicted to drugs is because they live with adult male drug addicts. We may not necessarily drive them to it, but if we keep putting it in front of them, us men can be pretty effective at drawing our loved ones into addiction. Makes sense really. If you lived with a coalman you'd probably have more open fires. According to Anglin *et al* (1987), when we stop having sex with each other, and opt for a little packet of powdery stuff instead, the rot has set in.

Male addicts and alcoholics tend to marry wisely, finding a partner who is sober enough for them both. The question then arises, what's in it for Mrs Clean? The most likely explanation is that the partner of an addict or alcoholic finds that they can feel easy around this person. As well as being infuriating, an active alcoholic or addict can be warm and charming and funny.

But the alarm bells can sound pretty early with addiction. Unreliability, a lack of cash, or conspicuous drunkenness on a relatively tame night out, all spell danger. At this point a would-be partner may fold and go find a more sober boyfriend. The woman who decides to stick around could be doing so because:

a)   She hasn't noticed anything abnormal.
b)   She has a purpose in life – to save this fella from himself.

In the case of a), her selective blindness may mean that this lady has a problem or two of her own (Okazaki *et al*, 1994), and so she engages in a spot of magical thinking (ie. ignore what's happening and it won't happen again). The addict is now perceived as a promising partner who is hopefully going to make everything right and bring her happiness. OK, so he collapsed, but those restaurant steps were steep.

Option b) is interesting. By dedicating her life to the salvation of a man, this woman is guaranteed a full-time job with opportunities to advance to sainthood. It's a two-way deal. Her alcoholic/addict boyfriend now has the chance to act with even less personal responsibility, as his guardian angel will clean up after him, apologise to all offended parties on his behalf, and phone in sick for him on Monday mornings. In exchange, she gets to feel like she's doing something genuinely worthwhile with her life. They fall in love and get married. If he then acts unreasonably (and let's face it, the chances are high) his understanding wife will understand. She'll scold him, indulge him, worry about him, watch him.

In a peculiar way, she is just as irresponsible as her husband, as she is not living her own life. Instead, she's living his. As long as he's happy, she's happy. Nice for the bloke, as it means that he can have what he wants. New clothes, computer, motorbike, whatever he's into at the time. The only problem here is that he has to be happy enough for two. 'If you're happy, I'm happy'. 'Great – lend us a hundred quid and we'll both be delirious. No, of course I won't spend it on drugs: what do you take me for?' In committing herself to rescue him, the addict's partner has trapped them both in an impossible fantasy: she'll control him and they'll live happily ever after.

The long-suffering wife believes that she's in control. She doesn't really drink, let alone take drugs, and she's a person who won't get depressed by life. Unfortunately, she's also a person who won't get elated by life either, which is probably one reason why she needs an addict partner. They can provide the fun. But she doesn't think she has any needs at all. She doesn't need needs. It's just that he needs her, and she loves him, so what's she to do? She's been denying her true or emotional self since her girlhood, acting as the 'doer' or the peacemaker. An addict partner provides a further method for her to follow her belief that all she has to do is control everything, and everything's going to be OK. Control everything – there's a challenge.

And in her mind there's no doubt, he must be controlled. Which is odd, as he was attractive enough to her when no-one was controlling him. In his mind there may be considerable doubt, but a discrete little drink will soon fix that. What she doesn't know can't hurt her.

Dr Frankenstein's experiment

If one partner is good enough for two, someone has to be bad enough for both partners. It appears straightforward, but in our relations we humans are generally more subtle and complex than good adult/naughty adult. A researcher, with the reassuring name of Dr Frankenstein and colleagues (1985), made the intriguing discovery that alcoholics made more positive statements towards their partners when they were intoxicated compared to when they were sober. Griffith Edwards and Jim Orford (1977) made a similar discovery when interviewing the wives of male alcoholics. The women said that their husbands were preferable to them drunk, as they then became more assertive. Of course there are plenty of testimonies to dreadful domestic scenes where one or both partners have been drunk, but the fact that alcohol can make a person more agreeable rather than less so can go some way to explaining why alcoholism is sometimes so hard to uproot within the context of a marriage or partnership.

If the alcohol begins to severely weaken her partner and reduce his effectiveness within the family, a woman may turn her attention towards her children, notably an elder son. Dad's sense of his own value would then really plummet. His drinking and general behaviour can be expected to worsen as his sorry decline continues.

Control

At various points the partner of an alcoholic or drug addict may decide that enough is enough, and either the addict quits or they're off. The partner will almost certainly try to give up, but the pressure's on. Deep down he or she will feel resentful, as giving up was not their idea. If the addict's heart isn't in it, a few dry weeks can seem like a decade, but their partner may show little recognition of the amount of effort that turning over a new leaf involves. Resentment and building tension can combine to the point where the clean and sober addict feels near bursting point. The choice is stark: either to continue with the miserable torture of stress and craving, or go and get out of it and blow the whole marriage. Unless... and so the ever-resourceful addictive mind sets about the task of secretly drinking or taking heroin or whatever. It doesn't matter that they got caught out last time – it won't happen again. The addict is once again looking to control his internal world (through chemicals) and control his external world (through deception). It's a very risky strategy, but it has to work.

Of course it can't work. How many years does the addict suppose can go by without his partner discovering? He doesn't ask himself this question as he knows the answer. In trying to control everything he is resorting to at least two options that are completely out of his control: his intake of mind-altering chemicals and fate. Sooner or later his luck's going to run out and everything will come tumbling down around him.

When an addicted couple make a pact to both give up, the result can be comic as well as disastrous. Cigarette smokers proudly tell one another that they haven't had a cigarette all day, then separately sneak off and beg a smoke from the same mutual friend, both swearing their bewildered mate to secrecy. An alcoholic woman I know agreed with her husband that they would both quit. Of course she didn't trust him, and in going through his wardrobe she found an opened bottle. She drank half of it, knowing that he couldn't challenge her about it because he'd already sworn that he had no drink in the house. She then went to her own secret hiding place in the kitchen, and was furious to discover that half of her bottle had been drunk by him. But what could she say? Chess is less complicated than the games played between two addicts in a relationship. Fals-Stewart *et al* (1999) made the intriguing observation that the longer some addicted couples both stayed off drugs, the worse their relationship became. This is a dilemma and no mistake.

Gay partnerships

Robert Cabaj (1992), estimated that gay men and women are three times more likely to suffer from chemical addiction than members of the straight community. I don't know why this could be true. Perhaps it's connected with having a personal lifestyle that's already against the rules. It may also be related to having more free time and disposable income, affording greater opportunity for misbehaviour. Or, in the case of gay men, the thought that boys together are not brilliant at maintaining sober conduct might be an explanation; we have a gender-based tendency to go down the pub.

Homophobia can't help either, so perhaps some gay people get out of it to shake off the uneasy feeling of being constantly watched and judged. To avoid the regulation of the straight world, gay men and lesbians often form their own societies, meeting in clubs and pubs where alcohol is generally on sale, causing further risk of addiction.

Thinking has completely reversed from the idea of one hundred years ago (see *Chapter 1, p.9*) that people become alcoholics and drug addicts because they're homosexual and they can't admit it. It's now half accepted that some people become addicts because they're homosexual and they can admit it. In declaring themselves free of the sexual conventions of society, some gay and lesbian people purposefully reject the regulation of other areas of their lives such as alcohol and drug consumption. We all love an explanation, and so this new way of looking at things is of some use. What is probably of greater value is the simple thought that gay men and lesbians are more vulnerable to addiction than the general population.

Children of addiction

Being brought up by alcoholics can be a poor foundation for a young person's life. When they reach adulthood, the children of alcoholics tend to suffer from a range of personal problems. Among these are difficulty with showing feelings, a tendency to feel over-responsible and a problem in trusting others. Male children are at a greater risk of developing alcoholism themselves, female children can go on to suffer from depression and addiction (Beletsis and Brown, 1981; Miller *et al*, 1990).

Many female children of alcoholics will go on to marry alcoholics themselves. Edward Kaufman (1992) suggested that a daughter of an alcoholic repeats this pattern because she believes that her mother did not love her father, and this lack of love caused him to drink. By truly loving another male drinker she will be able to save him from alcoholism, and in a way save her dad too, as in the mysterious recesses of our minds, the identities of our lovers and parents can overlap and merge. This all happens in the unconscious mind, beyond the reach of awareness. To the adult daughter, the fact that her husband appears to be developing alcoholism just as her father did is nothing more than an odd and unhappy coincidence.

There is also some evidence that children of heroin-addicted parents don't have the best start in life. Fears, insecurities and educational problems have been reported (Sowder and Burt, 1980). Some of the damage may have begun in the womb, and the presence of many drugs in breast milk presents an early threat to a child's physical and mental development. Without wishing to depress you, things tend to remain bad right through to adulthood. Problems in maintaining relationships, keeping on the right side of the law, and holding down a job are common themes. A great deal of this is learned, of course. Drug-using parents are outsiders – outlaws really – so difficulties their children might experience in dealing with the outside world can be expected. The child has to marry up two conflicting cultures, a conventional restrictive one called Britain, and an anarchic domestic situation that is addict family life.

Drugs are excellent at interfering with the way mum or dad actually feel about what is happening from day to day. That's why they take them. To a developing child, however, sudden and inexplicable shifts in their parent's mood can be very mystifying. We feel secure when we can predict what might happen next. Irrational outbursts, weird hilarity, incessant speech, depressed silence, loss of consciousness, frenzied activity: a few days in the care of a very 'druggie' parent can be puzzling and perhaps unnerving to a young mind.

As the years roll on the child makes the connection between the drugs and the changes in mum or dad's manner. They'll also catch on that unless they cook dinner, there's a chance that no dinner will occur. Mum and dad are still out to lunch. The child now becomes the little adult. The generations are reversed, with the parents stuck in a greying adolescence.

Alternatively, son or daughter may have to succeed where mum and dad have failed. The weight of expectation comes from the parents, who will tell Jade or Joshua that they've got a really good brain and there's no reason why they shouldn't do well. Jade may well want to do well – it keeps her uncertainties buried under a book and excuses her further interactions with mum and dad and their dopey mates.

In a home that's stuck under a cloud of an angry and dominant addicted parent (we'll say dad, to stereotype), it may be the job of the child to lighten the repressive atmosphere by playing the clown. It helps everyone to get through moments of gloominess or fear, but it means that Josh cannot be down himself. The family may come to rely on him to be the sunny jester, leaving the more serious part of him alone and unrecognised. In having to be 'up', it may be impossible for Josh to slow down and concentrate.

It's likely that these patterns get established in alcoholic families over the course of several generations. A neglected person will feel hurt or 'bad'. They can then jump to the faulty conclusion that they feel bad because they are bad. As they grow up, if there's one thing that they can't tolerate it's 'badness' in others – none of us can stomach strong reminders of our own weak-spots. This hurt adult has children, and when the children behave in a 'bad' way they criticise them severely: the reaction of wounded mum or dad is out of all proportion to the quality of the misdemeanour. The child, trusting the judgement of very big people, believes that the parent's criticism is justified. He or she now feels 'bad'. The child sees the solution – become a little angel.

All of these kids have become, of necessity and in differing ways, too concerned with the well-being of their parents. They have adapted themselves to the point where it's going to be very difficult to identify and tap in to their true selves when the demands of adult life begin to build. Separation from self and an early schooling in alcohol and drug use make us particularly vulnerable to addiction, and so the wheel turns.

There are a number of self-help groups for people who have experienced difficulties through living with addiction. Al-Anon, Alateen and ACoA (Adult Children of Alcoholics) are among the best known (see *Appendix*).

12
Addiction and a healthy mind

The persistent pounding of the brain with mind-altering chemicals is not the ideal route to mental well-being. The mind is thrown into confusion by the succession of waves of artificial messages that break over it then ebb away.

Our brain is designed to make some sense of what is happening to its owner. It does this during intoxication by just about keeping it together against all the odds ('I managed to find my way home – God only knows how 'cos I can't remember a thing'). If something really serious is happening our brain can often sober us up in an instant. At night our brain is busy assimilating what has happened in our lives earlier that day, re-enacting the big emotional moments in the form of dreams. While performing this very creative task, it will still keep enough of its wits about it to wake us up if there's an alarming noise going on. It's busy monitoring our world, working out what's happening, and letting us know when something is wrong.

To do all this, the mind must be vigilant. It has a demanding job, and submerging the poor thing in a pond of alcohol, or jolting it with blasts of crack cocaine doesn't help it in its work. Perhaps this in-built sentry duty function of the brain, the part that is always prepared to demand, 'Who goes there?' is at the root of some of the paranoic and aggressive outbursts common to addiction. The brain, under attack from a chemical weapon, senses that it must grab hold of a stick, but it's too befuddled to know which end of the thing to take.

Drugs certainly create emotions, including negative ones once the nice ones have worn off. Because the faithful bloodhound brain tries to find a reason for everything that goes on for us, it will snatch at the explanation that best fits the facts. The alcoholic husband may therefore judge that his wife and children deliberately upset him after he'd been to the pub at lunchtime. He was feeling all right until they started criticising him. The other members of the family will have a quite different version of events: dad came home drunk, crashed out in front of the telly, and the moment one of the children made a noise the old man went nuts. Alcohol's capacity to limit dad's reasoning power completes the unhappy domestic picture.

The brain can only take so much confusion, frustration and poisoning, and alcohol can drive us crazy in the end: the condition is known as Korsakoff's psychosis. As we've seen, some addictive stimulant drugs such as amphetamine can also drive their consumers mad. This may be due largely to a lack of sleep. If we don't sleep we can't dream, and if we don't dream we can't clear the emotional left-overs from the day before. The washing-up is not done and the sink piles up with dirty dishes. We start to overload mentally. This takes little more than five or six nights, at the end of which we begin to hallucinate. The undreamt dreams force their way into our conscious minds as they have no other outlet.

Dopey, sleep-inducing drugs don't carry this risk. Heroin addicts are often certain that they don't dream, which they quite like as it means nightmares are off the menu. They sleep well enough so I'm sure they do dream, but heroin has the capacity to separate people from fully experiencing what's going on. It can distance us from physical pain, it can block us from the emotional pain of unhappy events and, unsurprisingly, it can block our awareness of dreams. It is, after all, an anaesthetic.

Downers, like heroin and to some extent alcohol and tranquillisers, can injure our mental health by being simply that, downers. A flattening of our emotional life is not something we need year in, year out. There's that lovely warm duvet of pleasure in which downers envelope us, but as we've seen (see *Chapter 3, pp. 32–36)* this effect reduces over time as we become accustomed to the drug's positive effects. We might love a particular piece of music, for instance. We'll keep sticking the CD on, but eventually we'll play it to death, to the point where it gives us far less pleasure than a while back. Sadly, this does not happen so easily with negative experiences. We can, for instance, receive a huge phone bill and be far from happy about that. We can look at that phone bill every day for a month and still be deeply distressed at the sight of the thing. Downers have their own negative characteristics. Just as heroin can separate us from unhappiness, it can block us from experiencing the joy of happy events. This is why opiate addicts can appear so indifferent or world-weary. If you ask a heroin addict if she'd like to come down to the beach, she might say, 'What's the point? I'm happy enough here'. Be fair, they're not often to be seen sun-tanned and riding jet skis, although they might be attracted to an all-black wet suit. In a heroin-logic kind of way she was right though; if you are 'happy enough', why change things? But when do heroin addicts look happy? With longer-term use of downers, separation from the joys of the world persists, while the 'happy enough' state the drug always used to provide begins to drift out of reach. The addict has backed the wrong horse. Awareness on some level that things are progressively going in the wrong direction could be a factor in the tendency of heroin addicts to court death. Perhaps 'happy enough' isn't enough.

I hope I haven't depressed you at this point. To correct the balance I might say that at least you're not addicted to heroin. If you are, have you been to Bexhill-on-Sea lately?

To continue, the catalogue of bad things addiction can do to our minds are all possible from a starting point of relative mental health. We can come to addiction without a psychiatric problem such as depression or psychosis, but pick one up as a result of heavy drug use. More worrying still is the prospect of what might happen to someone who has a mental illness and then becomes addicted.

Schizophrenia and addiction

Schizophrenia, or what the world has long called madness, is probably the most disabling of all mental illnesses. The mind of someone suffering from schizophrenia is prone to attacks of paranoia, delusions and hallucinations. Because of the conflicting information about who he/she is and what is really going on around him/her, it's sometimes impossible for the person with schizophrenia to be sure of something as basic as their own identity. Things don't hold together, so a central 'me' or self cannot be consistently identified. It's a weird and horrible condition and there's no known cure. The fragmented components of the sufferer's personality can be glued together temporarily by medication known as neuroleptics. People who suffer from schizophrenia don't generally like taking these drugs as they can produce nasty side-effects. But if they don't take these medicines, insanity often takes hold again, and things can quickly get very messy.

So with schizophrenia there are two factors that make addiction a particular danger. The first of these is the precariousness of the personality. If you tend to believe that in reality you are Bonnie Langford and that the paper boy is transmitting psychic messages to you about an impending Lithuanian invasion, and that your brother-in-law is part of the conspiracy, then the last thing that might prove helpful to you is a mixed bag of street drugs. The second factor is the real messages that society sends out. Namely, that it's OK to drink and smoke, and – in the case of sufferers from schizophrenia – it's necessary to take powerful drugs.

In the nineteenth century alcohol was used in the spooky Victorian asylums as a means to dampen down the symptoms of schizophrenia. It was given to the patients as medication. Many people who have suffered with schizophrenia since then have discovered for themselves that alcohol can go some of the way to making them feel more integrated – less spaced-out. Alcohol is a pretty crude method of self-treatment. As mentioned above, too much consistent hard drinking can actually drive someone crazy, but it remains an attraction to a number of people whose lives have been blighted by this mental illness.

Nicotine addiction is also a real hazard to someone with schizophrenia. I don't know why, but this may well be due to the combined problem of the boredom of continual invalidity, coupled with an unwanted edginess that can be a side-effect of their medication. There's a double risk here in that the drugs used to treat schizophrenia can cause heart disease, as can cigarettes. I once worked with a young man who had schizophrenia. His liking for nicotine was so great, and his sense of social convention so slight, that he would smoke three or more cigarettes at the same time. He died from heart failure at the age of 33.

There are other addictive drugs that people who suffer from schizophrenia use. Tranquillisers (eg. Valium) can help to suppress some of the rogue thoughts that this mental illness can provoke. This type of drug has also been used by psychiatrists from time to time to treat schizophrenia, so it's not surprising that some sufferers are attracted to them when they come across them 'on the street'. Perhaps because they can be outcasts themselves, drug addicts tend to be tolerant of those people society usually rejects. This accepting and non-judgemental way makes it possible for someone with a serious mental illness to share their company and their drugs too. This may go some of the way to explaining why drug misuse is unusually common among people with severe psychiatric problems.

A group of drugs that are definitely not helpful if you have schizophrenia are the hallucinogens. Dope is a relatively mild hallucinogen, but it's still a bit of a brain twister and therefore potentially dangerous for someone with a fragile mind. Worst of all is LSD, which isn't really an addictive drug, but is still pretty popular and relatively easy to buy. LSD (or 'acid') manages to mimic the symptoms of schizophrenia in the minds of the mentally healthy, so it's potential effect on a person who is struggling against a psychosis can be catastrophic.

Depression and addiction

Being addicted to anything can be a depressing circumstance, and alcoholics and drug addicts are sometimes treated for depression by their doctor. I would hesitate to describe the majority of these cases as true depression. Unhappiness is probably nearer the mark. Addicts may not even disclose their drinking or drug-taking to the doctor, but simply report feeling low.

Depression proper, or clinical depression as it is known, is a profound kind of misery with a characteristic group of problems or 'symptoms'. These symptoms include a disturbed pattern of sleep with early morning wakening, poor appetite, and persistent depressed feelings. Someone suffering from clinical depression experiences a slowing down in their mental and physical functioning, to the point where they may become confused and slothful, as well as deeply fed up. As some of the symptoms of depression and addiction overlap (low energy, poor sleep, no appetite, low sex drive), researchers have found it hard to estimate what percentage of alcoholics and drug addicts suffer from depression. Results vary wildly, but by combining different surveys it's fair to say that male alcoholics and addicts are twice as likely to be suffering from depression than non-alcoholic men, and female alcoholics and addicts are three times more likely to have an underlying depression than women who do not have a drink problem.

Some depression sufferers have turned to drugs to escape from their problem. Alcohol, as I've suggested, is quite a commonly used chemical prop. It seems to provide temporary relief, but regular drinking does more mental harm than good, and people who are depressed and drinking heavily represent a high suicide risk (Schukit, 1986). Drinking can certainly prolong depression (Mueller *et al*, 1994), and because alcohol is a depressant, heavy regular drinking can of course create depression. This is like non-chemical depression in every respect except that it lifts soon after the drinking stops.

Stimulants, such as amphetamine and cocaine, have also been tried by people troubled by depression. But what goes up must come down, and the low that follows the high from using an upper can be bad enough if you were in reasonably good spirits when you approached the launching pad. If you were already depressed at the point of take-off, the eventual drop can be a desperate experience. In fact, in cases of severe depression there's evidence that cocaine doesn't make users feel any pleasure at all (Post *et al*, 1974).

Opiate addicts are also prone to depression. The sedating quality of this group of drugs can sap natural vitality; and perhaps the main reason why heroin and methadone addicts can suffer from depression is no more complicated than the fact that they are trapped by their drug habits. As a rule, research shows that the worse the habit, the greater the chance of depression (Latkin and Mandell, 1993; Dackis and Gold, 1992). But, of course, this fact doesn't prove that serious addiction is the cause of depression. It's equally possible that depression can be the cause of a serious addiction. Someone who has long been tormented by negative emotions could find their deepest cares evaporating with their first taste of heroin. A number of heroin users I've worked with have related this sort of unburdening experience. They've used words like 'cocoon', 'blanket' and 'bubble' to describe the insulating and protective effect of the drug. It's not too hard to see how addiction might follow. Any of us could probably get addicted to not feeling desperate.

The common denominator between addiction and depression is a feeling of hopelessness. The addict feels hopeless because their drug has taken away their freedom. The person with clinical depression feels hopeless either as a reaction to some very upsetting knock-backs in life, or because his or her brain is mystifyingly deficient in the manufacture of uplifting brain chemicals. Whatever the route, the destination is the same. The ways out of these problems differ slightly. It may be necessary for someone with a true depression (ie. one not caused by drink and drugs) to take antidepressants for some time after they've stopped using alcohol or whatever their poison is.

Anxiety and addiction

Anxiety among addicts is probably more common in females than males (Brady *et al*, 1993). It's an uncomfortable state to be in. Anxiety can be sub-divided into a few categories. Generalised anxiety describes those of us who worry about everything and anything (arriving late, arriving too early, forgetting things, the house falling down, etc.). Free-floating anxiety describes people who are tense and on edge, but can't specifically say why. On the other side of this scale is phobia. Those among us with phobias have very specific anxieties around a single object or event. Fear of heights (altophobia) for instance, or fear of confinement (claustrophobia).

In their extreme form, anxiety problems can be crippling. People become swamped by irrational fears to the point where their hearts beat like crazy and they feel like they're either about to collapse or die. These panic attacks are unusual, but people who have experienced them are often willing to try anything to prevent them from happening again: drugs, for instance.

Quite a few drugs are good for anything from mild worry to nasty anxiety states. Nicotine's not bad, alcohol is first class, heroin is very good and tranquillisers are marvellous at reducing tension and worry. These drugs are also very addictive, so that someone who uses them for their anxiety-reducing properties as well as for straightforward fun, is running a double risk of addiction.

Just as what goes up must come down (see 'Depression and addiction' *p.105)*, it's probably equally true to say what goes down must come up (unless it's the Titanic or Sheffield Wednesday). Anxiety that has been held clamped down by drink or drugs can come bursting to the surface with renewed force once someone stops taking whatever they've been taking. The chemical lid has been removed. This upsurge in anxiety has to be ridden out before a period of calm can be reached. In the case of alcohol and tranquillisers, the charge of nervous energy can be so extreme that it's not physically safe to go straight from addictive intake to zero (Morse, 1999). A gradual tailing off needs to be arranged, and this should be done with the help of a doctor.

Coming off alcohol and tranquillisers may not be such a tragedy for the anxious person. Although initially they're great for steadying the ship, with consistent use these drugs begin to falter in their ability to calm frayed nerves. Eventually things can reverse, and the drink and pills can actually make the consumer more nervy instead of less so.

This is a dreadful stage in alcoholism. The alcoholic feels incredibly over-sensitised and vulnerable. The slightest event, such as a knock at the door, or the most innocuous thought, such as 'my sister is due to visit today' can send the advanced drinker into a tailspin of panic. All he knows is that he must have some vodka to keep from going mad. To remedy the problem he turns to what caused it. He knows what he's doing, but if the present is intolerable, we do what we must and disregard tomorrow. The alcoholic has no other solutions as he has narrowed and fashioned his life around the solitary strategy of drinking for all reasons.

There's no fun now – the drink is taken solely to get through to the next awful day. This is end-stage alcoholism. Shakes, palpitations, panics, horrific hallucinations (often featuring insects) and episodes of memory black-out are all common. Addicts and alcoholics can also enter a kind of anti-spiritual inner world. Here fear and panic progress to terror, and a distinct sense that the addict is in the presence of evil. It may be no more than the imagination of a tormented brain, but a number of people I've worked with have reported having this dreadful experience. One man, Dan, told me that his drink and drug addiction had taken him over totally. Trapped and alone, Dan turned in his room to find the devil sitting at the foot of his bed. The devil gave him a mocking gaze and said, 'What are you going to do now, boy?' I don't know that Dan did anything, as this was an unusually worrying development in his drug career. What I do know is that he was not really the religious type, and that he didn't really like repeating the story as he knew most people wouldn't believe it.

Post-traumatic stress disorder and addiction

It's now widely accepted that there's a psychological condition that troubles some people who have either either been a direct victim of, or have been close to, horrific events. Post-traumatic stress disorder can plague sufferers for years after something dreadful has happened to them. Car crashes, violent attacks, catastrophic fires and many other such traumatic incidents can reverberate through the witness's mind. This persistent distress can take the form of nightmares, sudden flashes of fear or rage, deep sorrow, or a persistent sense of guilt at being one of the 'lucky' survivors. A high number of adult post-traumatic stress sufferers turn to drink and drugs for some peace of mind; addiction becomes an obvious hazard (Keane and Wolfe, 1990). The situation is complicated and worsened by the fact that living an addictive lifestyle brings someone closer to the possibility of further horror. Brutal beatings, drunken attacks and sexual violence can all occur in places where the standard social rules have broken down. To numb the effects of these monstrous events (which in turn can re-activate memories of past horror), someone with a post-traumatic stress disorder may slide further into addiction.

Other psychiatric conditions

Bi-polar affective disorder may cause those people who are unfortunate enough to suffer from it to seek relief through drink and drugs. Bi-polar affective disorder used to be called manic-depression. It's a disabling see-saw of highs and lows. The high 'manic' phase sees the sufferer in a very excited, elevated state of mind. He or she needs little food or sleep, and is distracted by almost everything encountered. At this point the sufferer is highly impulsive and has an impaired sense of danger. These characteristics can combine to make over-consumption of chemicals a real possibility. Someone in this aroused state may also turn to drink and drugs to calm their over-stimulated mind. They may equally use drugs to extend this manic episode, which may be chaotic and damaging, but often features very gratifying feelings of omnipotence. The low or depressed phase is the opposing wave of the cycle. This bleak episode may last for several months, during which time heavy drinking is a particular danger.

The standard treatment for bi-polar affective disorder is a drug called lithium carbonate. Lithium is fairly poisonous, and it doesn't make the safest cocktail when mixed with street drugs.

Part II
Addicted, what now...

13
Giving up

Addiction is a craft, and full-blooded alcoholics and drug addicts are its masters. The drinker can track down a bottle at three in the morning in a strange town. He can be the centre of attention, delighting those in his company with hilarious and extraordinary tales culled from decades of good living. He can convince almost anyone that he's hardly drinking at all, while he calmly drifts from one secret drink store to the next. The drug addict has a pharmacist's knowledge of drugs, a barrister's knowledge of the law, an accountant's head for figures, and a politician's gift for lying himself out of any tight corner. For addicts, drink and drugs are an occupation as well as a preoccupation. It's a lot to give up.

Alongside all this is the knowledge that he or she could last 'out there', in the world of addiction, for a while longer. The addict has survived so far, and once this tricky patch is over, well... It may be dangerous, but it's familiar and, as I've said, the addict is a master of his or her class, part of the elite of the drinking and drugging nation.

Then there's the question of having had quite enough already. This goes against the instincts of any true addict. Sometimes they're in hospital before they've had enough. So giving up is a very foreign concept.

The positive advantages to giving up drugs may be difficult for a dedicated addict to see. The addict will have great unease about taking the plunge and finally quitting. Improvements in relationships, health and standards of living may seem distant and doubtful. There's also a kind of hopelessness that develops when addiction really has its teeth set in to us, and things can appear distorted through this defeatist lens. The addict may not feel that they've got what it takes to beat this thing. This leaves little room for manoeuvre, but two handy tactics are, 'I'll quit tomorrow' and, 'I can give up any time I like'.

I'll quit tomorrow

Giving up tomorrow buys the addict some time and places faith in the idea that on another day he or she will have the mental strength to stop. It also leaves a potential escape route for addiction the next day, as tomorrow can bring all kinds of uncertainties, any one of which can be blamed for obstructing the true and righteous march towards clean living. The budgerigar may suddenly go off its millet, and the worry of this can be enough to make it essential to smoke or take heroin.

It's not just bad things that can keep us entrenched in addiction. If an old friend calls by and he or she is a hard-core smoker or drinker, the potential 'quitter' can be lighting up or knocking back a beer before they know it. At this point (that is to say once the cigarette has been lit or the drink has been drunk) the frustrated addict will look in mock dismay at the object of his or her obsession and say, 'I was supposed to be giving this stuff up today! Oh well... Fancy another?'

It's not acknowledged that the would-be 'quitter' had virtually dragged their mate into the house. They might even have phoned them up to ask them round in a thinly disguised game of, 'Let's sabotage what I know I've got to do'. Plus there's the potential guilt of abandoning a friend by leaving the diminishing band of smokers and heroin users. Given the choice between doing something agreeable like the taking of drugs, and something disagreeable, like stopping the taking of drugs, it's small wonder that any addict takes option number one. They can always give up tomorrow.

I can give up any time I like...

The truth may well be that any addict can give up any time they like. At this point the outside observer can fairly ask, 'So what's all this addiction stuff? I'm wasting my time reading this stupid book!' The answer to valid criticism like this lies in the language of the addict. Of course the addict can give up any time he likes. The fact is that he doesn't like to give up. And he probably never will like to give up. He likes the drug. It's nice. He likes it so much he's made it the centre of his life. I can give up foreign holidays and sex any time I like. Would I like to right now? Thank you but no. Would I like to in the future? Almost certainly no. If my life depended on it?

The writer F Scott Fitzgerald believed that he could take alcohol or leave it. This meant that he had a choice and he, rationally enough to his own mind, decided to take it. It's impossible to say whether he had a real choice not to take it but he died early following a long alcoholic decline. Narcotics Anonymous' simple observation is probably right:

> *Most addicts resist recovery, even when they*
> *want it.*

NA, 1988

Rather than giving up any time I like, the problem with giving up becomes, 'Can I give up any time I need to? Suppose my wife says, "Either you stop drinking or me and the kids are off?" Or the doctor tells me,"Stop or you'll die".' I take a long hard look at my options and I decide that I need to stop. I must stop. But I find I can't – the pull of the drug is just too strong. It's time to call in the experts.

Relapsing back into addiction

The first thing to be said about relapse is that it happens. It happens not just to addicts, but to everyone who has ever drunk enough to get ill, groan 'Never again', and gone on to repeat the same mistake. Relapse happens more frequently in the early months of quitting, when the addict finds himself in the very vulnerable situation of having plenty of fresh bad habits (which may include getting up late, not working, leaving problems until they get considerably worse, drinking copious amounts of alcohol, taking stacks of drugs, not being incredibly honest in relationships etc.), and a limited supply of good habits (brushing teeth, being polite to old women, eating). If the addiction has been catastrophic in its effects, then it's possible that even these basic standards of behaviour have not been consistently maintained. In short, things have been seriously out of control.

There may be a shattered family that can never be the same, serious debts, the loss of a home and the unshakeable feeling that in the great game of life the addict has landed on the longest snake on the board. The picture looks grim. It's enough to make you want to drink, which of course is the one thing you cannot do, and the one thing that got you into the mess in the first place. That said, do people relapse because they feel so depressed by what drink or drugs has done to them? A straight yes or no answer is not possible.

As Davies (1997) points out, when we ask someone why they relapsed we assume that they have the answer. It can be as upsetting and as mystifying to them as it is to those around them; all that good work wasted, and a dreadful feeling of going into some sort of emotional and social free-fall. They drop like a stone and their friends may drop them like one too. One man I worked with chanced a pint of lager on Friday night. By Monday morning he was back to his old habit of a bottle of gin a day. For others the return to addiction can be a gradual slide over the course of two or three years. Besançon (1993) interviewed 31 alcoholics who had given up drinking only to start again. On average it took them 13 years to go from their first drink to the point of alcohol addiction (the morning shakes etc.). The average length of time it took them to return to full-blown addiction was just seven days. Only three drinkers managed more than 30 days of control drinking, although one of these three clocked up almost six years before succumbing again to alcoholism.

One of the horrible ironies of addiction is that people sometimes slip back into drug use because they are happy rather than sad. The result of interviews between Alan Marlatt (1987) and some addicts who had returned to their habitual drug use, showed that the third most common reason for relapse was that the addict was in a good mood! Just as being down can make us view things in a distorted negative light, being happy can make us too positive and unrealistic about the way things stand. Presumably someone can get caught up in an atmosphere of fun and relaxation and let their guard slip, assuring themselves that they're in control and just one drink/joint/line won't hurt. Addiction doesn't care how well and confident you feel. To most of us happiness is happiness. To addiction, happiness is opportunity.

Other factors that can trigger relapse include social pressure. Heroin addicts are particularly prone to the influence of friends and associates, presumably because their mates are always using heroin (Daley and Marlatt, 1992). Smokers are also at risk, maybe as a consequence of the unhelpful, 'Go on, have one' generosity of other smokers. Alcoholics are less likely to take a drink as a result of social pressure. This is not surprising, as there are fewer occasions during the day when people might offer you alcohol, rather than nicotine or heroin (depending, obviously, on the company you keep).

Family support can play a significant role in protecting someone from slipping back into alcohol or drug addiction. It's less of an influence on smokers. They tend to go back to the cigarettes for largely emotional reasons – feeling stressed, down or upset (Catalano *et al*, 1988).

In recent years a method of treatment known as relapse prevention has become popular among professional helpers (Gorski, 1995; Marlatt and Gordon, 1985).

14
Alcoholics and Narcotics Anonymous

Alcoholics Anonymous started from a chance meeting in 1935 in Ohio of two reforming alcoholics, Dr Bob and Bill W. The funny names were to protect the identities of the drinkers from the stigma of the outside world. Stigma's still big today, so first names only remains an AA imperative. Dr Bob (Bob Smith) and Bill W (Bill Wilson) found that by sitting in the same room and engaging in conversation, two alcoholics together could manage to do what they couldn't do alone: not drink. They decided to spread their happy discovery among alcoholics they met. Most didn't want to know, but the idea began to slowly catch on.

Meanwhile, other Americans were pursuing the possibility of sobering up by turning to religion, something that has long been a feature of self-cure from alcoholism (Cutten, 1908), or by 'going into therapy'. Carl Gustav Jung was one of the foremost therapists, or 'analysts' of the first half of the twentieth century. He had tried manfully to keep an American patient called Roland H from drinking, but all Dr Jung's methods had ended in failure. In frustration, after a year of private consultations, he told drunken Roland that there was nothing more that psychiatry could do for him. His problem was spiritual rather than mental, and it would take God or some bloke like Him to stop him drinking. I don't know what Roland said in reply, but for at least an instant he must have experienced that uniquely individual sensation of having been thoroughly ripped off (Kutz, 1979).

Roland decided to get spiritual and went to join a religious set called the Oxford Group. They had a system of self-improvement based on Christian principles that Roland followed, and he found to his surprise and delight that his drinking stopped. Other alcoholics also had some luck through joining the Oxford Group and adopting their methods.

Eventually, Roland and other sobered-up members of the Oxford Group met up with Dr Bob and Bill W. The result was the incorporation of a spiritual system, or 'steps' into the approach of AA. These 12 Steps were based on the notion of power. They said that in essence alcohol is stronger than an alcoholic. However hard he or she tries to do to beat it, they will lose. To survive, the alcoholic needs to shift the balance of power in his or her favour, and to do this they need to enlist the help of something or someone more powerful than themselves. God's a very good start. Follow the instruction of God or another 'Higher Power' and you'll have the personal strength you need to beat the drink.

At this point AA began to take off, and membership has grown from two men in the thirties to over one million today. To provide a similar service to drug addicts, an off-shoot organisation called Narcotics Anonymous (NA) was formed in California in 1953. This was not a favourable era in which to be identified as a junky (Burroughs, 1954), so meetings had to be especially clandestine. NA built its approach to addiction on the AA 12 Steps, substituting the word 'drugs' for 'alcohol'.

Enlisting the help of a higher power sounds promising, but it requires at least two leaps of faith. The first is to accept the belief that you can't beat alcoholism on your own. The second is to put your power and trust in some abstract idea. The first three of the 12 Steps spell out this method:

1. We admitted we were powerless over alcohol and that our lives had become unmanageable.
2   [We] came to believe that a Power greater than ourselves could restore us to sanity.
3. [We] made a decision to turn our will and our lives over to the care of God as we understood Him.

These three sentences are dense with ideas about addiction.

In Step 1 the word 'admitted' carries the implication of owning up and surrendering to the undeniable fact of addiction. 'Powerless' means no power, no resistance. You take another drink, and you will look on helplessly as your life slides back into horrible chaos, or 'unmanageability' as AA call it. AA uses another piece of pocket wisdom to describe the alcoholics precarious situation:

One drink is too many, one thousand isn't enough.

For an organisation that was born in Ohio, AA can be very Zen.

Step 2 says that after waving the white flag in Step 1, an alcoholic has to look outside of him/herself for solutions. This ties in with the psychological theory of addiction that says that the addict/ alcoholic is encased within him/herself, endlessly searching for the way to feel right about themselves and destined to be unable to find this unrealistic state of ease or serenity. Meanwhile, the gramme of coke and three bottles of wine are making things less serene by the day. This trait to look for something else (ie. a drug) that will make things better can be used to positive ends by making that 'something else' a spiritual entity (ie. God).

Step 3 is packed with concepts that are very pertinent to addiction. Making a 'decision' is not easy for an addict or alcoholic. They generally defer decisions until they've had a hit or a drink. After that, the decisions can get a bit unrealistic and hard to recall. An alcoholic can make a decision to drink several pints of lager, but it's unlikely that this is purely an act of free will. Addiction is leading him by the nose. He may be lead by members of his family in the opposite direction, towards help from doctors and counsellors. He may even stop drinking at this time, but he has not made a 'decision'. He can drink again if he chooses because he never decided to quit in the first place. AA and NA know all this.

Step 3 also talks of turning 'our will… over'. Addiction has long been described as a disease of the will: you want to resist, your will is to resist, but you can't resist. The solution is simple. If your will is defective, give it away. If you don't have it, it can't harm you. In a sense an addict has already given his or her will away to the dealer and the drug; the alcoholic has donated his will to Smirnoff. 'Care' is an interesting word, suggesting the replacement of one big carer (the chemical security blanket) with another, every bit as powerful (Mr God). Step 3 shuffles a short distance away from Christianity by letting AA/NA members define their own God, but it's reassuring to patriarchs everywhere that He still remains a 'Him'.

AA or NA help to keep their members off their chosen poisons by providing regular meetings. Members can substitute a bad habit (going to the pub) with a healthier one (going to an AA meeting). The format of these meetings is remarkably similar across the globe. First, the chairman calls the meeting to order by introducing himself by his first name and declaring himself an alcoholic. He then reads a statement that spells out the function and purpose of AA. A speaker is then called, who again declares his first name and his addiction. He will tell his story – the early years and the first taste of drink, the struggle with alcohol, his moment of defeat and the turning point it inspired. There's no cross-examination, but when he is finished others are free to introduce themselves and compare their experiences to his own. Further speakers may tell their stories and more sharing of experiences is likely to follow. References to AA philosophy and the 12 Steps are common. The meetings close with a short prayer.

There are two or three reasons for this structure. Firstly, addiction can be a very repetitive, almost ritualistic, activity; addicts can feel at home with the predictable. Secondly, AA and NA are the products of Western Christian culture, with its emphasis on the value of confession. The tradition of repentance goes back through 160 years to the Washingtonian movement, an organisation that had brief but spectacular success in restricting alcoholism across America. The Washingtonians held public meetings where encouragement was given for what they called, 'experience sharing' – an expression that now sounds strangely modern (White, 1999). A third purpose for this AA and NA agenda is to meet the addictive need to make something happen, to have a powerful experience. By talking openly about personal matters, members can have this desire met. AA or NA meetings can act like a drug by changing an attendee's mood; he or she goes to a meeting feeling tense or generally out of sorts. They leave feeling enlivened or uplifted.

AA and NA do not concentrate on the question, 'Why am I an addict/alcoholic?' The answer is beyond reach, as this book sadly demonstrates. The mystery of addiction is left as just that, and instead, these Anonymous fellowships focus on what is to be done about it. The message from AA philosophy is that addiction is not an addict's fault: he or she has been suffering from an involuntary illness.

This removal of blame by-passes a large area of the emotional minefield of guilt and shame. The alcoholic can begin to unburden himself of the shame he's been carrying since he arrived drunk at an important social event, insulted the host, and collapsed over the finger buffet. The guilt the addict may be experiencing for stealing money from his family and generally being an unmitigated disappointment over the years is also relieved. Great. Now comes the second part of the AA message. You are not to blame for your addiction, but you are responsible for it. You have an illness and you've got to do the right things to control it. This is quite tough reasoning. How can you be responsible for something that isn't your fault? You might as well take responsibility for the fall of the Roman Empire, or the concept of Monday mornings. There's no denying that this personal responsibility idea doesn't hold up too well to logic. But this doesn't over-worry AA and NA members. Of greater concern is the distinct possibility of death. If the house is burning down, you don't stay in it and debate the cause of the fire.

Emrick (1987), in looking through dozens of research papers on the effectiveness of AA, calculated that half the people who commit to long-term membership clock up several years on the wagon. Approximately two thirds of long-term members improved to some extent. The figures are impressive, but of course there are thousands of alcoholics who don't become active members of Alcoholics Anonymous.

Griffith Edwards found evidence that people with the most serious alcohol intake, such as two bottles of spirits every day, tend to benefit from AA, provided they turn up (Edwards *et al*, 1987). This matches my own working experience. In talking to clients about how they came to start drinking again their answer has frequently been, 'Well I stopped going to [AA] meetings a few months ago. I thought I was alright, but…'. What Edwards also discovered in his interviews was that those members of AA who went to meetings who both gave and received support faired better than members who tended to be only on the giving or the receiving end of things. It's possible that people who find themselves unable to play this twin give-and-take role conclude that AA meetings can't really help them with their devastating problem, so they eventually stop turning up.

AA love an aphorism or saying. 'One day at a time' is one of their classics (tempering the addictive urge to have everything right now). They also love a paradox, perhaps because they're as puzzling as addiction itself. One particular AA piece of homespun philosophy is, 'We keep what we have by giving it away'. Sounds daft really. If I had a cheese sandwich and I gave it to someone else, I wouldn't still have it. But AA is concerned with something much more important than sandwiches. If an alcoholic has concern for himself but he transfers that concern to those around him, he manages to attract care or concern in return. In the case of hope for the future, by talking encouragingly to others the alcoholic keeps up his own spirits. As people we can drag each other up as well as down. I particularly like 'Giving up and winning', as it applies not just to the act of quitting to win a new life, but also to a method of finding a solution to a maddening problem by stepping back from the struggle. At least, that's what it means to me.

The position it takes on addiction – you are an alcoholic, you will always be an alcoholic, you can never drink again – is hard to misinterpret. This gives protection against the kind of double thinking that can occur in addiction (for example, 'I've managed to cut down so much that I'm entitled to a good drink once in a while').

This stance has frequently been criticised for being too rigid and fanatical (Bean, 1975). All the time the addict or alcoholic is not taking drink or drugs he remains on the right side of the fence. If he slips up he is back in the clutches of addiction. He is also separated from the companionship of his chosen club. And, having failed to successfully use his higher power, he is in spiritual disarray. At least that's probably the way that the disappointed addict feels at that moment. AA and NA philosophy can be very harsh on those that can't keep straight or sober, but the message is tempered by an announcement that is made at the start of every fellowship meeting across the world; that the only precondition to membership is a desire to stop drinking or taking drugs.

AA and NA do not suit all alcoholics and addicts who are in the act of giving up. Most AA members are men, so an exclusively female organisation, Women for Sobriety (Kirkpatrick, 1978), provides a valuable alternative. The Anonymous movement's reliance on God has been too much for some addicts to swallow, and they've gone on to create Atheists Anonymous and the Secular Organisation for Sobriety. Cultures that aren't based on Old Testament values have instigated their own self-help organisations, for example, Danshukai, or Japanese Sobriety Association.

15
Getting help

Helpers

Asking for help is as abnormal to an addict as not drinking or taking drugs. He or she may from time to time ask for money, not to be sacked or kicked out of the house, but it's a highly unusual moment when they request real at-root help with their problem.

Now I am not an alcoholic or a drug addict. There have been periods in my life when I haven't denied myself the odd drink or drug, but currently I don't go for anything stronger than a nice cup of tea. But if I were to become addicted to drink or drugs I wouldn't go to see someone like myself for help. I might get a few facts and figures from him, but I'd soon make my excuses and find someone who really knows what it's like to be addicted: a former alcoholic or drug addict. This is because the facts and figures I'd have been given by someone like myself would make it clear that this is the wisest course of action. Stinson *et al* (1979), for example, found that help provided by alcoholics who were 'on the wagon' was more effective than programmes run by doctors and nurses. Galanter *et al* (1987) found similar results when they followed a pub-full of alcoholics through two different programmes: a conventional clinic-based treatment, and a self-care programme that featured support from volunteer sober alcoholics.

After some years in the trade I am convinced that a reformed addict is better at helping someone to change their life around than a professional non-addict. Obviously there are exceptions. If, for instance, the reformed addict spends half of every counselling session whistling the melodies to the hit musical Cats, then suggests that his touching your genitals would be a very positive therapeutic activity, you'd be better off with someone like me. I hate Lloyd-Weber's work. A more serious potential exception comes in the form of the highly zealous counsellor who is emphatic that the method he followed to clean up is the only way for any of his clients to overcome addiction. There are a number of roads that lead to addiction, and there are probably more than one road out.

Veach and Chappel (1990) tried to find out why a reformed addict is of more use in dealing with addiction. They interviewed 962 doctors who had no declared addiction problems, and 307 doctors who identified themselves as recovering alcoholics or addicts. They found that the 'former addict' group were generally less judgemental, less pessimistic and less liberal in their attitude towards addicted patients. This combination of toughness, optimism and broad-mindedness is – in my opinion – hard to beat when it comes to helping an alcoholic or drug addict.

Getting help: caution

I believe that a lot of alcohol and drug workers are a bit too fond of mind-altering chemicals themselves, and in finding employment in the field of addiction treatment they are making a living out of a fairly deviant hobby.There have been times in my working life where this profile has matched me. If there's one thing that makes you feel easy about yourself, it's being around people who are in a worse state than you are. It's also nice mixing with people of similar habits and outlook, like going down the local or visiting some burn-out mates. And if you're getting paid for doing it, well, so much the better.

Professionals who are no healthier than their clients are no new problem. In 1978, Pursch reported on a two-week alcoholism training programme for 475 doctors. At the end of the course 9.2% of those who attended turned themselves in for alcohol treatment.

So can a 'counsellor' who may have a problem controlling his or her own drink/drug intake help a client who honestly admits to having a similar problem? Unlikely, you'd have to say. But, on the other hand, how close an understanding can be struck up between a streetwise heroin addict and a retired bank manager who, other than a glass or two of sherry at Christmas and weddings, has never had anything stronger than aspirin in his life? It's not exactly going to be a meeting of minds. No, the counsellor should perhaps have walked on the shadier side of the street himself, otherwise the addict will struggle to relax and talk openly. A reformed drug addict or drinker is the best possible helper. Retired poachers generally make the best gamekeepers, and addicts who have climbed on the wagon know every excuse and trick as they've used them all at some time in the past. The addict is disarmed by the insider's knowledge of the been-there counsellor, and is thus unable to protect the addiction.

Getting help: realism

How is getting into a conversation – however earnest – with another person really going to help anyone to get better? The idea that two people (an addict and a therapist) can go into a room and come out again after an hour, and that what has occurred in that time can permanently change the addict's life seems to have more to do with voodoo than science. The would-be counsellor who enters the people trade with the expectation that he or she will be able to sort somebody out, in some way 'fix' them, is setting their sights far too high.

It's not possible to change a person. They can only change themselves, and that in itself is a monumental task which may be beyond their reach, despite all their best efforts. Other than addicts, few people in this life have to try to change. Their lives don't depend on it. But the happiness and survival of an alcoholic or drug addict may be impossible without real change.

Treatment

Bruce Johnson and John Muffler (1992) have pointed out that every drug user who goes for help has a unique blend of problems. The chances of their meeting someone who can give them exactly what they need to iron out all these difficulties must be somewhere between extremely remote and non-existent.

The most important question regarding addiction treatment is, 'Does it work?' The answer is, if it's good treatment offered by dedicated experts, it can work for some people for a short while. This falls a long way short of, 'Yes: 100% cure guaranteed every time', but we have to be realistic – addiction is a stubborn condition that pesters its victim from one year to the next. People ask for treatment because the best efforts of the sufferer and their family have failed to beat addiction. Sustained resistance to it takes a tremendous concentration of time and energy, because addiction is a part of its victim, it's intrinsic to them. To think of cure is to miss this point – we can never be cured of being ourselves.

What do the surveys tell us? A fair answer can be reached by considering various studies and coming up with some average statistics. Miller and Hester (1986) took on the laborious task of sifting through over 500 pieces of research into the treatment of alcoholism. They found that on average, over 75% of the drinkers were back on the drink within one year of treatment. Chad Emrick (1974), in an epic piece of bedtime reading, worked his way through 384 studies of alcohol treatment. His figures for relapse were well over half in the first 12 months after treatment. The first 90 days appear to be particularly risky.

The year that follows treatment sees many alcoholics slip back into drinking. A similar pattern emerges for heroin addicts and cigarette smokers (Catalano *et al*, 1988).

On the surface these are depressing facts. What these studies sometimes don't tell us is the level of drinking or drug use that people resettled to following treatment. It's possible that it was lower. There may also be some improvement in the client's relationships. And, an apparently 'failed' attempt might help someone move closer to cleaning up further down the road. This trend has been noticed in some well thought-out research studies (Hubbard, 1992).

Treatment works for some people and not for others. Those people who seem to do best have comparatively few social problems, a limited range of drugs that they regularly use, a supportive home environment, a job, a partner who does not use drugs, good mental and physical health, a good education (Vaillant, 1983). In short, enough things going their way. Giving up drugs can make your life easier, but it can't get you money and a nice new home.

A famous piece of research into whether treatment of alcoholism works or not was carried out in England by Griffith Edwards and Jim Orford (1977). They randomly divided 100 married men into two groups of equal size. Group A was given a typical alcohol 'treatment', involving individual counselling and group therapy, in-patient treatment if they needed it, and counselling for their wives. Members of Group B were given half-an-hour's advice and then left to their own devices. Twelve months and 24 months after these 'treatments', Group B's members were drinking no more than Group A. We can be fairly sure of this fact as Edwards and Orford had the good sense to ask the men's wives as well as the men themselves how much and how often they'd been drinking. This result suggests that advice is as valuable as treatment. Or even that treatment is no more valuable than advice. It also demonstrates just how resilient addiction can be. Addiction counsellors have to be realistic and com-passionate, and careful not to run away with the idea that they're curing anyone.

When things don't work out as hoped we generally ask whose fault this must be. Are the people who offer this treatment to blame?

After all, they put themselves forward as experts in the curing of addiction. Mental plumbers, in a manner of speaking.

Previous generations of experts have offered some pretty questionable help to alcoholics and drug addicts. Infusions made from deadly nightshade, high voltage electrical zaps through either side of the skull, bits of the brain surgically sliced, or the injecting of enough insulin to bring on a coma. Even strychnine's been tried (Linstrom, 1992). These all might be considered mistakes of the past. Of course we've got it right now. Don't worry.

There are a number of different kinds of treatment out there these days, and I don't intend to play one off against the other and say, 'In tests, this brand proved to be the most effective in fighting all known addictions'. The plain fact of the matter is that treatment does quite a few people some good in the short term. In time the effect of treatment lessens. After two or three years there is often no real positive effect noticeable for the majority of addicts and alcoholics who have been through a treatment programme. Their drinking and drug-taking is on a par with a similar group of people who had no treatment during that time (Linstrom, 1992).

Does this mean that treatment is a waste of money? Shouldn't we just leave addicts to their own reprehensible devices? Or, more economical still, follow the opinion of Richard who fixes my car, and shoot them: ('Why not, they're no use to anyone, not even themselves?'). Well we could do that, but it would mean a fairly radical change in legislation. A treatment that might help someone to clean up for a year or two or perhaps 15, has tremendous social value. Children are happier when dad's off the gear, the roads are safer as soon as someone stops drinking and driving, we get robbed less often when there are fewer of our citizens hooked on heroin or crack. The NTORS (1999) project has calculated that for every pound we spend on treatment here in the UK, we save three pounds in reduced theft.

One form of treatment that does appear to have long-term benefit for alcoholics was devised by a man called Nathan Azrin (1976). His idea, like all good ones, was simple: let's just make it as difficult as possible for an alcoholic to drink. To do this, he involved all major elements of life. Employers were involved in the treatment, as was the alcoholic's partner, and representatives from the alcoholic's preferred 'sober' activities. If the alcoholic had no job, one was found, if he or she had no sober social activity, a desirable one was set up. Azrin then got all these key figures in the drinker's new life to agree to be supportive for as long as he or she did not drink. Drinking would result in swift pre-arranged withdrawal of help. Finding him or herself surrounded by a vigilant and co-ordinated ring of people, the alcoholic drank less. The drawback to this system is that it costs a large amount of money and depends on the right kind of client – a poorly educated young drug addict with no work experience and no partner is unlikely to be helped by a system that was designed for a middle-classed professional alcoholic. However, there is some evidence that an adapted programme can help heroin addicts (Abbot *et al*, 1998). What Azrin's work teaches us is the value of engaging all of the support that can be brought together for anyone looking to build a new life.

Treatment, in the short-term at least, is probably a good thing. I'll qualify that by saying that good treatment is a good thing. Bad treatment is a total waste of time and can be even worse than that. There are some ethically unconventional counselling practices going on from time to time, with therapists sleeping with their clients, or using drugs with them, or both. Not exactly the sort of help the taxpayer had in mind when they forked out good money for a dedicated expert to rescue members of our society from the misery of addiction.

The potential 'patient' needs to be careful in selecting a therapist or group of therapists who can be trusted. Once an alcoholic or drug addict has become satisfied that they are in the hands of someone with integrity, trust begins to build. This is a very nerve-wracking time for a person with a serious addiction problem, as life may have taught them that if they trust anyone they'll end up getting badly misused. But they have to take the risk of putting their lives in the hands of another person: with addiction your life is hardly safe in your own hands.

And so begins the alcoholic's or addict's scary task of looking into the deeper, darker corners of him or herself. Now whether the person who helps the addict to do this works in one kind of way such as cognitive-behaviourism, or another system known as motivational enhancement therapy, doesn't really matter. Someone once said that the longer two specialists work in their own very different ways of treating people, the more similar their methods become. Very wise words. I wish I could have remembered who it was that said them.

Anyway, the bottom line is: Is The Therapist Any Good? The addict has to put faith in this person or group of people. He or she needs to believe that they can show them how to get off drink and drugs, as they don't know how to do it themselves.

Trust is a vital starting point, but next comes the ability to help the addict to relax and start talking. Valle (1981) found that some counsellors managed to help their alcoholic clients to keep off the drink better than others, and that these more successful counsellors had 'higher inter-personal skills'. In other words, they were easier to talk to.

Not that talking is the beginning and end of therapy. I believe that someone could be helped to overcome serious addiction by an acupuncturist or a spiritual healer. Words aren't everything – we existed before we knew any language at all, and to a great extent it's not the actual words that are spoken that carry the punch in therapy, it's the feelings that they convey. If these same critical feelings can be experienced as a result of a prick with a needle or the touch of a hand, the job can be done just as successfully without the need for questions and answers. But again, it's down to the quality of the therapist. I could stick a pin in your foot and call it acupuncture, but you wouldn't thank me for it and you'd be cured of nothing.

Individual counselling

This is harder than it at first appears. Someone wants to come off drink or drugs, so they see a counsellor. The counsellor says, 'Don't get drunk', the client says, 'Don't worry, I won't', leaves, and gets drunk. Things can go on like this for months or years. So the counsellor changes tactics and says, 'Tell me if you get drunk', 'OK', says the punter, leaves, gets drunk, comes back and says, 'I got drunk'. 'Oh', says the counsellor. It is progress, but hardly a monumental advance.

As drinking or drug-taking is an activity, a thing that people do, it can be measured. Unfortunately, much of the measuring must be done by the client. This is a bigger problem with alcoholism, as drinkers often play down the amount of drinks they've had. Non-alcoholics do it too, talking about going out for a 'swift half', or having 'a couple of drinks'. Somewhere down the line we all must have got the message that drinking is wrong. Unless further prescriptions of goodies from the doctor, or their future liberty depend on it, drug-takers don't tend to under-report their drug use. They're usually quite open about how much they've taken, how they delivered it into their blood stream, and how much they paid for it.

Assuming we've reached a point where the addicted 'client' can now trust his or her counsellor with the facts about the amount of drink or drugs they're taking, and also assuming that this addicted 'client' has decided that it really is time to pack it all in, we are now down to the nitty gritty of individual addiction counselling. The counsellor – I'll say she's a woman – has to hold on to three things:

1. Her nerve, as the client is heading into uncharted territory, and may get to feel very uneasy at times.
2. Her hope, as the client may not initially believe that recovery is possible, so the counsellor needs enough belief for two.
3. Her instincts as the client may be on the verge of relapsing, or might even have done so, but is too afraid to speak about it.

Addiction counsellors each have a style of their own, but they can be tough when it comes to getting to the heart of the matter. They're an odd mixture of compassion and ruthlessness. No matter which way a client turns, their counsellor will be in pursuit, tracking down any addictive thought or action with a steady and remorseless flow of questions. The addiction counsellor appears to be constantly analysing things, and when a client asks them why, they'll probably say something like, 'Why do you ask that?'. There's a sort of mental tug of war that can go on between the counsellor and the client, the purpose of which is to pull the client out of the grip of addiction.

There are two basic ways a counsellor will try to do this. The first relies on an idea that goes back to Roman times: thoughts cause emotions. What we are thinking influences how we feel. What's more, how we feel often dictates what we do. It relates quite neatly to addiction. For instance, a client may think that no-one really cares about him. As a result, he feels fairly unlovable and rejected, so what he does is get grossly slaughtered. Someone with an active addiction can find it very difficult to work out the differences between thoughts and feelings. They may have become addicted mainly to get away from all that thinking and feeling business. They could therefore respond a bit too literally to questions based on this way of seeing addiction: 'What did I think? That I could do with a hit. How did I feel? I felt like a hit. So what did I do? I went and had a hit'. The counsellor now has a golden opportunity to earn her money.

The other popular method of addiction counselling looks at what an addict is trying to achieve. What does he or she want? How are they currently going about getting it? People usually resolve to give up chemicals because they want fewer problems and greater peace of mind (McMahon and Jones, 1993). It's fair to say then that an addict's strategy for living (get out of it as often as possible and deny everything) has a practical flaw or two. Be that as it may, the counsellor still holds the view that the client had a higher goal in mind. This could be anything from the creation of a happier home life, to the building of a career in journalism. By frequently asking how their current attitudes and habits help to bring them closer to their goal (eg. happier marriage, job on *The Times*), the counsellor tries to help a client to find out a more realistic and less chemical route to their nominated destination.

Individual counselling for a woman with an addiction problem may have to cover all sorts of related problems. These areas might include the impact of sexual abuse, practical and personal child-care difficulties, and a drinking or drug-using partner. Low self-worth is a distressingly common theme to female addiction, even among women who appear full of confidence and good-humour. Much of the therapist's work may be centred on trying to convince a female client that she actually deserves to get better and take her place in the world. The focus on treatment of men, by comparison, tends to be on the outward signs of distress such as anger. To state a rule that is so general as to be of almost no value, I would say that women turn their distress in on themselves in the form of self-blame, while men tend to push it out in the form of blame-anyone-other-than-self.

The thing that unites all individual counselling sessions is the question of , 'How to stay off'. Some therapists will focus on the clients emotional well-being, in the belief that someone who is relatively 'in-tune' with themselves will have some protection against relapse. Other counsellors concentrate on thought patterns, teasing out 'old' addictive ways of looking at life. Addiction can be very subtle. George Christo (1998), found that a failure to avoid drug-use environments was the most common cause of relapse among the drug addicts he had interviewed. On one level these addicts may have had no conscious intention of going back to drugs, but things were probably working under the surface, making chance swing in addiction's favour. Before they knew it, they found themselves in the same room as a pipe of crack cocaine. One side of the addict's mind had managed to out-manoeuvre the other.

16
Staying off

Once an alcoholic has dried out, the job of the counsellor changes considerably. They must now help the alcoholic to stay dry. This kind of work is called relapse prevention, and it can be divided into three areas of the drinker's life. The first is the learning of new ways to deal with the outside world. The counsellor might want the drinker to learn some new tricks in greeting and chatting with people. The purpose of this would be to help the reforming alcoholic to feel more relaxed and confident in social situations. Previously, he always had the support of the nearest bar when he needed some Dutch courage. Now the drinker must stand alone.

He can feel nervous in company, and the counsellor might work with the alcoholic to reduce these anxious feelings. The work can entail things as simple as remaining near the door and breathing more slowly, to identifying the client's worst fears around a social event, and testing the likelihood of the imagined disaster actually occurring ('everyone's going to stare at me and I'm just going to lose it ').

The counsellor may also encourage the client to take a look at problems with anger. Once the lid of drink or drugs is removed, feelings can come spilling out all over the place. I've even heard it suggested that reforming addicts can develop an unhealthy habit called 'rageaholism' (Bradshaw, 1997). Outbursts of anger can be quite pleasant in a way – you can experience a volcanic release of tension, allow yourself to lose control, and feel completely blameless because it was all someone else's fault. If it's true that someone can get pleasure from anger, a counsellor is unlikely to change things. An addict or alcoholic can get as angry as they like provided they don't drink or take drugs. Danger may come if their anger pushes other people away, making support less likely and, as a consequence, relapse more of a risk.

Like the anxiety counselling, this anger work ranges from the straightforward ('when you feel yourself getting wound up, sit down') to the complex ('Are you really just angry, or are there other more difficult feelings underneath?'). This deep and meaningful stuff is certainly worth a look. Men are only meant to have a couple of emotions – happy enough or angry. Inadequacy or loneliness are discounted, but they exist all the same. As these are both negative emotions, we only have one door they can pass through – anger. A good counsellor can help an addict to spot these more subtle emotions and build a plan to cope with them.

In our culture women are definitely not permitted to get angry, which must make them angry straightaway. What women are allowed to be is sad or depressed, or in some other way angry with themselves. Angry with themselves for eating too much, for instance, or for being a 'bad mum'. One-to-one counselling with female addicts who have cleaned up will often focus on this low opinion women are allowed to develop of themselves, or self-anger.

Assertiveness training is also a significant part of the treatment game. It's more usually done as a group activity as opposed to individual work, so I'm not sure why I've included it here. Assertiveness is supposed to help addicts not to feel too put upon. If they don't say no to unreasonable demands, a recovering addict can become over-burdened and resentful and tired; a sure relapse recipe.

Some counsellors will tell their clients to plan for a relapse. It's a bit pessimistic, but if you go out with an umbrella it usually won't rain. The plan may involve carrying a card with names and phone numbers of people who could be of help. The message is that a slip is not a catastrophy, or, 'a lapse doesn't mean a relapse'. This is difficult ground for the addict. There's generally a side to addiction that tends to deny the scale of the problem ('things haven't been that bad; I'm not like that now'), and the thought that a lapse can be accommodated and successfully dealt with may play right in to the hands of addiction. After all, it's the same mind that created the addiction that would be playing with the idea that it can be controlled next time. It's a little like giving Dr Frankeinstein back the keys to his laboratory, or handing an arsonist a box of matches. They both may have learned from their misadventures, but…

A brilliant counsellor may even be able to spot a relapse coming. They will certainly be advising their client on how to read warning signals which may begin to appear days or even months before any chemical is taken. The drug can be the final brick in a wall that there is building around the client. Increased secrecy, a return to old ways like lying in bed, cutting off from helpful friends and resources (such as the counselling sessions themselves), and the growth of a resentful kind of gloom are among the worrying signs. I've spoken to people who have vividly described this horrible pattern. They've watched their own demise like some helpless spectator. They've told me that they have often considered killing themselves in preference to losing the gifts that months or years of addiction-free life have brought. These reported experiences more than any other have convinced me that addiction is a real thing rather than a myth created for and by professional people (Davies, 1997).

It's a cause of great woe that people lose their foothold when they've climbed so far above addiction. One reason often given for falling off the wagon is that it can be a pretty miserable vehicle that doesn't seem to reach appealing destinations. Although free of drink and drugs, the recovering addict can find him or herself stuck in an ongoing rut of low moods. Martin and Jasinski (1969) called this mental cul-de-sac the 'protracted abstinence syndrome'. But giving something a name doesn't help matters. Alcoholics Anonymous offer the biblical reassurance, 'This too shall pass', which I take to mean, hang on in there because things will get better. Hanging on in there is a position familiar to alcoholics and addicts who are trying desperately to stay on the wagon. They call it 'White Knuckling'. Looking to more hopeful times is not an addict's strongest suit. When the present feels unbearable to an addict, it can become exactly that. It's great to live in the moment, except when the moment is unbearable. Not even 'one day at a time' seems to answer this one.

Alcoholics Anonymous have another of their ready mottos for the avoidance of relapse:

> Don't get too hungry, angry, lonely or tired.

Not ones to waste ink or complicate an idea, they've condensed the advice further, into the pneumonic HALT. It's good solid advice, and it also connects with an unusual addiction theory belonging to Janice Keller Phelps:

> *All addictions arise from the same underlying cause – an error in metabolism that creates an abnormal hunger.*
>
> Keller Phelps, 1986

Controlled drinking

Most UK citizens who drink practice controlled drinking. They don't get too drunk too often and they haven't suffered many problems as a result of their drinking, such as losing their driving licences, getting the sack, or ruining their health. Drinking patterns across many countries show that there isn't a split population of light drinkers and heavy alcoholic drinkers (Edwards *et al*, 1997). The graph doesn't suddenly jump from a few drinks per week to two bottles of vodka per day. It looks more like a kid's playground slide, with a steep climb from zero to two or three drinks per day, then a smooth diagonal descent through five, ten and twenty drinks. It peters out at 40 or more drinks, as beyond this consumption people die before they have a chance to fill out the questionnaire. This pattern of drinking remains true for countries where the drink is scarce (Norway, for example), and for nations where alcohol is cheap and plentiful, such as France. The difference between the two nations is found in the height of the slide. In France five or six drinks per day is the norm, whereas the average Norwegian adult has one or two. As a result, the French have the worst livers in Europe.

There are occasions in the lives of many people when their drinking is not too well controlled. Men in early adulthood often drink too much. Or someone who has been bereaved or made redundant may drown his/her sorrows to the point where people become quite alarmed. These periods of heavy drinking usually resolve themselves, sometimes with the help of a counsellor or doctor. In cases like these it would be perfectly reasonable to aim for a return to normal, 'social' drinking. This is a desirable strategy for two reasons. First, social drinking is normal – over 80% of UK citizens do it (Edwards *et al*, 1997). Second, if the person who is looking to control their drinking fails to do so, despite trying every known method, they now have some personal evidence that their addiction is a relatively serious one. If they had been engaged in social drinking, it was in the guise of a highly gregarious newt.

But the difference between social and alcoholic drinking is not clear-cut. Alcoholics do not generally drink alcoholically every day. George Vaillant (1983) measured the intake of several men with severe alcohol problems. He found that in a typical year they only got drunk on 180 days. Similarly, if you were to monitor the drinking of a number of social drinkers over the Christmas holidays, many of them could be mistaken for alcoholics. This is great news for true alcoholics, as they can reason their problem into non-existence by highlighting days when they've been as sober as a Methodist judge, or explain that they're drunk because they've been celebrating the Philippino New Year in Huddersfield.

The methods recommended by counsellors to drinkers who are trying to cut down are a mixture of common sense and psychology. The 'client' is encouraged to keep a diary of their drinking, and to go through the details with their counsellor. Obviously, 'Monday: Got Pissed', won't do. Times, places, company kept, and quantity consumed, are all necessary facts. The counsellor will be looking for patterns. Certain times of the day may be identified as more risky, some friends emerge as less helpful than others, and so forth. A plan will be drawn up which puts new healthier pursuits in place. It's hard to drink heavily in a Spanish for Beginners class. Some old drinking mates may have to be avoided, and refusal techniques may be set as homework (eg. 'No thanks; three's my limit').

The psychology comes with a more personal kind of diary. The client may be asked to divide each day's page into three vertical columns. The first column is titled, *What happened,* the second, *How I felt about that,* and the third, *What I did.* There are variations on this system, but let's stick with this one. The client may enter under *What happened* an event such as 'I argued with boss'. In the *How I felt* column he or she may write 'Wound-up', and in the *What I did* section they put, 'Went home and drank two bottles of wine'.

The purpose of this exercise is to try to get a heavy drinker to look at connections between how they feel and how they act. In the fairly simplistic example above, there may be all kinds of neighbouring influences that came into play. The client may have rowed with the boss because they were late for work due to the previous night's wine. Or a very drunken friend may have visited them after their return home. It's the job of the counsellor to sort the wood from the trees and help the drinker to identify potential triggers to their drinking. If the counsellor is a good detective, they can follow the clues: 'Did your friend just drop by? Oh, I see, you phoned them when you had got back. Where did the wine come from? You bought it on the way home. Just in case'.

There is all sorts of work that can spin off from this deceptively simple example. Would it help if the client learnt some new tricks on how to deal with argumentative people? Or ways of dealing with stress or worry? It probably wouldn't do any harm, and the thought that he or she is taking positive action to reduce the risk of heavy drinking can be beneficial in itself.

Controlled drinking training has been shown to help reduce the consumption of drinkers who have mild or moderate alcohol problems (Sanchez-Craig and Wilkinson, 1987). The bigger question is whether training in controlled drinking can help a proper shake-like-a-spin-drier alcoholic to join the ranks of the social drinker. The answer is usually no, but a famous study by Linda and Mark Sobell in 1973 reported that twenty severe alcoholics had learned to drink socially. A lot of experts were sceptical about the truth of the results, to the point where accusations of fraud were made. An ugly court case followed, but the verdict did not appear to satisfy anyone. Doubters believed that the temptation to move from, 'just have one more then', through, 'Oh alright, but this is positively the last', to, 'Oh sod it – I'll tell the wife I was kidnapped', would prove irresistible.

The 20 alcoholics whom the Sobells had taught to drink sensibly, were tracked down ten years later by Pendery *et al* (1982). Nine of them were reported to be back to drinking to excess, four had sadly died, and six had quit drinking altogether. Only one of the twenty was still drinking normally. Having devastated the Sobells' prize-winning sandcastle, Pendery and his friends stomped on the one remaining turret by concluding that their solitary success, (the lone social drinker), had never been an alcoholic in the first place.

There's little doubt that the Sobells' clients were helped to control their drinking for the first year following their training/ treatment. An alcoholic or a drug addict can feel that their treatment is working. They can tell their therapist that treatment is working. In fact, it is working. But a year or so later the addict is back to drinking or drugging again. Why? Because they are an addict, and that's exactly the kind of thing addicts do. What helped yesterday, helped yesterday. We don't stop eating because we've already had meals in the past, and for someone with a severe addiction problem, regular on-going support can be as vital as food.

Social drug-taking

This is another very popular national pastime. The number one illicit recreational drug is cannabis. Dope smokers tend to smoke it every day, but they rarely ask for help, other than to get out of their armchair. This is probably because dope's not too expensive, so a habit isn't a huge economic problem. One drug that does create problems for a number of its admirers is heroin. Much of a drug counsellor's workload is concerned with trying to help heroin addicts to control their problem.

There are some heroin users who don't generally touch the stuff during the week, reserving their pleasure for the weekend. They are practising their own method of controlled drugging, and there would be little advantage to their seeking outside help. But many heroin users take the drug on a daily basis, and unlike alcohol, going a few days without heroin once you've become a regular user, is not an option. Even reducing daily intake can be an uncomfortable experience.

The rehab

The concept of the rehab is far from new. In 1810 the American Dr Benjamin Rush recommended special treatment establishments that he called 'Sober Houses'. This was an idea of considerable humanity, well in advance of its time. Unfortunately, Rush wasn't always on such good form. Another of the treatments he recommended strongly for alcoholics was to give them a good hiding (White, 1999).

Modern alcohol and drug rehabilitation centres originated in Minnesota in post-war America. They represented a meeting point between two quite different addiction schools of thought: the self-helpers and the professionals. The self-help camp was composed of members of Alcoholics Anonymous; the professionals were the medical establishment – doctors and psychologists. One of the first rehab programmes was developed by a psychologist called Daniel Anderson, at the Willmar State Hospital in Minnesota (Anderson, 1981). It was based on the rather gloomy principal that addiction to alcohol is a disease for which there is no cure. The best that can be done is to keep off drink and other mind-altering drugs for good, thereby ensuring that the disease doesn't worsen to the point of death or insanity. The Minnesota approach introduced recovering addicts and alcoholics as counsellors, working alongside the more traditional doctors and nurses. The doctrine of Alcoholics Anonymous in the form of the 12 Steps, and the use of group therapy formed the backbone of treatment. 'Patients' stayed in the rehab for between four and twelve weeks. Minnesota rehabs operate in many countries today. Clouds House and Broadway Lodge are two well-known UK centres. Hazelden, which opened for business in Minnesota in 1949, is still flourishing in the USA.

One of the advantages of rehabs lies in their straightforward and clear philosophy: you can't control addiction as long as you are still dabbling around with drink and drugs. The way to do it is to stop everything completely. This idea couldn't be simpler – you cannot be addicted to drink and drugs if you don't take any. According to the abstinence way of thinking, if you do go back to taking a bit of this or a bit of that, sooner or later you'll end up taking a lot of this or a lot of that and be in as big a mess as ever.

This fundamental idea that addicts shouldn't have anything because they'll soon lose control once it's in their systems has been challenged. One very interesting piece of research measured how many fluid ounces of different drink alcoholics consumed (Marlatt *et al*, 1973). Some of the drinks contained alcohol, and others didn't. The alcoholics were misled by the researchers, who told them that the non-alcoholic drinks were alcoholic. Alcoholic drinks were presented as alcohol-free. The statistics showed that where the alcoholics believed that a drink contained alcohol, they were more inclined to get stuck in. When they felt that a drink contained no alcohol, they would drink less (only half as much). What this research suggests is that a chemical may not in itself dissolve an addict's ability to limit their consumption. The addict also has to want to get drunk or stoned. Laberg and Ellersten's (1987) research, however, appears to contradict Marlatt *et al's* findings.

Therapy is all very well, but it can't cure you from addiction. Despite the hundreds of hours you may have spent in dealing with the pain of how your dad never really paid you any attention, or exploring how and why you couldn't adjust to life after the family moved to Milton Keynes, if you decide to risk a swift half on the way home don't be surprised if you wake up 16 pints later in your neighbour's garden shed, feeling like you've been run over.

Which is odd, because rehabs give you untold lumps of therapy. You are encouraged to talk about your early life and your current relationship and how you feel right now, and all the rest of it. The full psychic re-fit. Sounds like a contradiction, but there is a reason for all the soul mining along with the straight up and down, 'You're an alcoholic and there's no changing fate'. It's that diseases flourish in unhealthy conditions. We get sicker in the cold and damp. If addiction is a kind of mental disease, someone suffering from it needs to keep their mind as healthy as possible. By working on painful memories some of the power of these things from the past may be reduced. The addict is facing some of his or her demons, making his inner world a safer place. More *at ease*, less *diseased*. Return to addiction becomes, in theory, less likely.

As Nick Heather and Ian Robertson (1997) point out, the idea that the sickness of addiction has taken over the controls of your mind as soon as you pick up a drink or a drug can be very depressing. It can cause the addict who has made the slip-up considerable panic. In this state he or she might believe that they've blown it and total chaos is inevitable. The thought can then occur, 'So why not let go and just go for broke?' The 'Addiction is an Illness' idea can't be infallible. It is just an idea. Although someone may have been addicted to drink and drugs for a number of years, we don't know if he or she will be able to use chemicals in safe moderation in the future. It's unlikely, but there's always a chance. That chance, it seems is around seven in a hundred (Finney and Moos, 1981; Pettinati *et al*, 1982). The disease idea, therefore, has the ability to scare an addict away from taking a foolhardy risk with a drink or a drug, but it also has the capacity to frighten the pants off the addict who does make a mistake.

Education

It's probable that most alcoholics and drug addicts know that they are engaged in an unhealthy activity. It's equally possible that they're not over-bothered by this. As a culture we might come up with statements like, 'As long as you've got your health, you've got everything', but we act as if deep down we know that's rubbish. We eat unhealthy foods, we don't take enough exercise, we do stressful jobs just for the money, and we consume toxic chemicals. Education about the dangers of drinking alcohol and using drugs have had little influence on the behaviour of the Great British public. The consumption of street drugs has rocketed over the past four decades, despite grave health warnings. The amount of alcohol we drink seems to have far more to do with how much it costs and how much cash we've got, rather than with how much information we've received from the government about our livers.

When addiction kicks in, one of the lesser priorities in maintaining a habit is the need for a healthy lifestyle. If an addict does respond to education, it's generally within the limited but specialist subject, 'Where can I get a drink/more drugs in Saffron Walden at two in the morning?'.

Despite these obstacles, alcohol and drug workers often provide health education to their 'patients'. These lectures are not simply along the negative lines of, 'If you carry on the way you're going your leg might fall off'. They can be quite sophisticated but practical sessions aimed at showing the audience new ways of dealing with the everyday hassles of life without the necessity to carry on the way they're going (and risk their leg falling off). The subjects range from coping with stress to making a college course application or how to inject drugs more safely. There is quite strong evidence, particularly among alcoholics, that much of this educational work is ineffective (Miller and Hester, 1986; Sanchez-Craig and Walker, 1982). The number one problem is memory retention (Becker and Jaffe, 1984). Years of hard living does the grey matter no favours when it comes to storage of new information. And concentration isn't all it could be during the early days and weeks of recovery from addiction. It should also not be discounted that members of the class can secretly be drunk or stoned. We have to be realistic.

A further possible explanation as to why education given to addicts doesn't appear to work lies in the thinking behind the teaching. The 'lessons' are given on the presumption that addiction will respond to reason. If we find some rational new ways of dealing with our lives we won't need to take drugs and drink. The truth might be that we can learn new social skills like how to make a public speech without panicking, or how to argue a point and not explode. We can take in these handy, rational tips, but get drunk anyway. Addiction has it's own logic.

Preventing young people from becoming addicted to drink and drugs is a separate area of health education that I don't intend to examine. What I would say is that programmes are often classroom-based, focusing on self-value and the right to refuse to go with the crowd. Sadly, the people most at risk of developing addiction would probably not be in school to take part, as truancy is a common theme in the early development of addiction.

The therapeutic community

It sounds like the sort of nightmare Kafka might have had after winning an international stilton-eating contest. The worst way to spend a year anywhere you could name. The therapeutic community. But I've met people who have found the experience agreeable. Only yesterday a man called Mark told me that the six months he spent in a therapeutic community were the most important and the most fun of his life.

The first of these communities opened in California in 1958, and by the 1960s they were beginning to prove effective in the reduction of heroin use among former residents (DeLeon *et al*, 1982). Therapeutic communities are generally large houses where addicts live together for several months under the supervision of former addicts. They were founded to address heroin addiction in particular. Their guiding philosophy is that heroin use is part of a lifestyle that involves the addict assuming an image. They are playing the part of a bad boy or girl. Many therapeutic community residents have had problems with authority outside of their drug use. A proportion of these will have been in gaol. This rebel image (Collison, 1996) needs to be dismantled if the addict is to be able to resist future offers of heroin from other street rebels.

Although it features the quality of regularity, drug addiction is not a very disciplined method of living, so therapeutic communities put emphasis on work and responsibility. Full commitment to the community brings its own rewards, and residents can rise through the ranks to achieve greater independence. The final stage may involve moving to a smaller shared house or flat, with minimal supervision.

Aggression, slacking, negativity, and drug talk are not tolerated, being regarded as the potential signs of addiction. Easy options such as constant television are also discouraged – the addict has to learn to take pleasure from the simplest things in life such as feeding the chickens, cleaning the house, hill-walking, and playing daft party games. The street glamour of heroin or crack addiction is given little purchase.

Unlike the system in rehab, group and individual therapy is not given centre stage in the therapeutic community. There are group meetings, but their purpose is primarily to settle the kind of arguments that are inevitable when several adults are forced to live together for months on end. They are therapeutic in the sense that residents use the meetings to challenge one another's recent behaviour, and behaviour is at the root of addiction. These meetings are no place for the faint-hearted, and the counsellor who conducts them has to be tough and skilful if things are not to get out of hand.

One criticism of therapeutic communities is that they only target drug addiction. Alcohol is not regarded as equally bad, and after leaving the community a resident is free to drink socially but still regard him or herself as being free of drugs. Some communities allow weekend visits to the pub. Critics may say that this carries a risk of alcoholism, or future drug addiction, as the 'loosening' effect of alcohol may weaken resistance to other drugs. There is limited evidence to back up this view (Del Pozo *et al*, 1998). The therapeutic community movement is more of the opinion that a former resident has learnt a new way of living that doesn't include the attitudes and values of drug addiction. They should therefore be protected against alcoholism, and deserve the rewards of social rehabilitation in the form of a pint now and then.

Some therapeutic communities welcome alcoholics, but they aren't allowed to drink, which must be a frustration to them. They're probably not allowed to take heroin either, which would suggest some bias in favour of the drug addict.

Therapeutic communities offer a place for someone to find a new (street) drug-free way of living. Their strength lies in bringing people with a shared problem together to support one another. At a time when an addict is trying to do the hardest thing in his or her lifetime, and self-belief and belief in others may be at its lowest, communal treatment gives him or her the opportunity to do something for someone else. Makes a refreshing change from letting them down or ripping them off.

Behavioural

As we've seen, alcohol and drug addiction runs in families. Parents and other relatives unwittingly school the coming generation in the over-use of chemicals, who in turn train the next generation. They also teach their children how to talk, how to blow their noses, and perhaps how to drive a car. None of these lessons is lost – they all become an established part of a developing person's vocabulary or behaviour. We don't forget them and we don't have to re-learn them (try teaching yourself how to drive again to test this idea – it's a very unnatural and awkward procedure). So, what we've learned is in-built and is done without almost any thought or planning. Little wonder then that addiction, once learned, can be so hard to change.

Behavioural treatment is treatment that looks at this ingrained pattern, and tries to break the almost automatic consumption of alcohol or other drugs.

To break the chain of thinking about or seeing a particular drug and then taking the thing, some alcohol and drug workers have tried showing images of drugs to an addict and then not giving them the drug. An alcoholic, for instance, would be shown a picture of a delicious glass of lager, but would be offered no beer. A heroin addict might be shown pictures of the drug and maybe of people engaged in the preparation and taking of heroin. Again, the treatment would involve the heroin enthusiast not receiving any of the substance.

This form of help is based on the idea that being exposed to a drug without actually getting it serves to break the habit in practice. This works quite well in other areas of human activity. A cook, for instance, is surrounded by food all day, but constant working with food without consuming it may tend to reduce the cook's appetite. The idea is most severely tested when, say, an alcoholic is flooded with images of drink in a day-care clinic, then leaves to go home, encountering pubs and off-licences on the way.

Another approach involves rehearsals of risky situations. In what is often called role play, the addict is offered an imaginary drink or drug. They then have to say, 'No thanks, I've given up' or, 'No thanks, I don't want another one'. At the same time the addict may need to check his right arm, which is shooting forward towards the offered drink, his hand curved in the perfect outline of a glass of Guinness. The trick here is for the refusal to come as naturally as possible from the addict. It's also useful to thoroughly close the door. 'No thanks, I'm trying to give up', probably won't do, as it gives a cue to the undermining, 'Go on, one more won't hurt', response that the half-drunk amateur addiction specialist so frequently gives. 'No thanks, I don't drink' is quite a good one, as pub and party-goers don't generally crave the company of teetotallers and will soon make an embarrassed exit, as though they'd just propositioned a plain-clothed nun. The alcoholic should not perhaps employ this 'I don't drink' strategy when conversing with someone they know well. Hilarity can be offensive as well as enjoyable.

Other than dealing with the person to person, 'Do you want a drink?' problem, the addict also has to get clever at working his way out of more general tight spots. What does he or she say, for instance, when they are out in a group, and everyone agrees that they should all go on to a nightclub? Or what's to be done when the addict is at a dinner party and after the pudding all the drugs start coming out? To someone without an addiction problem it's perfectly simple: 'You lot carry on – I'm off'. But these words tend to stick in the throat of a habitual drinker or user. The thought and sight of their favourite things can hold them hypnotised. Every trained fibre in his or her body demands that they stay. Before they know what's happening, they're striding up to the bar or expertly rolling up a bank-note, all good intentions safely dispatched. A new set of automatic speech and action has to be learned.

Make no mistake, this is extremely hard. If, for instance, you were told that you must learn a new language and never use your mother tongue again, your task would be similar in dimension to that of a true alcoholic or addict who attempts to give up. Now imagine that you are a year into your totally Norwegian-speaking lifestyle, and you're hanging a picture of some fjord or other up on the wall. You miss the nail, and the hammer hits you full force, smack on your thumb. What language do you swear in? It might only take one bad second to undo so much good work.

Alternative therapies

Complementary therapies are very useful as part of an all round treatment programme. A soothing massage with oil of dandelion and burdock will probably not be enough to keep someone off drugs. But there's plenty of personal testimony to the value of the healing arts when it comes to helping with the discomfort of withdrawals.

Following a discovery made in 1972 by Dr Wen of Hong Kong, acupuncture has been known to ease the pain of opiate withdrawal. The anti-opiate drug naloxone has been found to block the beneficial effects of acupuncture (Mayer *et al*, 1977), so it seems more than likely that acupuncture is closely involved with the body's endorphin system. Acupuncture and TENS machines (those little black boxes that deliver an electrical pulse to the wearer) are now widely used across the world to help opiate addicts to detoxify.

Reflexology is also gaining acceptance, and there is evidence that it too can ease opiate withdrawal pains (Sumption, 2001).

Chemical

A very straightforward method for stopping addiction in its tracks is the taking of something which makes the addict's favourite drug either very unpleasant or useless when consumed. The idea goes back some time. Around 100 years ago an alcohol 'vaccination' was patented. Made from the blood of horses that had been fed on alcohol, 'Equisine' was applied to the scarified skin of alcoholics (White, 1999). It didn't work too well.

The next leap forward came with the introduction of a drug called disulfiram or Antabuse. Antabuse works by interfering with the body's method of breaking down alcohol. If someone drinks after taking an antabuse tablet, the alcohol remains only half-digested, in the form of the very horrible by-product acetaldehyde. The hapless alcoholic is then violently sick and wishes they hadn't bothered. Antabuse has helped a good number of alcoholics, but it isn't effective for all. Some people find that they can drink without any adverse reaction, others don't drink for as long as they keep taking the tablets. But addiction, being as determined and as crafty as it is, somehow arranges it that the prescription runs out when the drinker is miles from the nearest chemist but next door to a well-stocked pub.

The alcoholic's partner often supervises the daily taking of the pill, but this needn't be a huge problem to a resourceful drinker, who can either hide the thing under the tongue or dive off to the bathroom and bring the tablet back up before it's digested.

In recent years a drug called Naltrexone has become popular with doctors working with heroin addicts. Naltrexone grabs hold of areas of brain cells which are normally the target of opiates. This leaves the heroin or codeine or methadone to kick aimlessly around the blood stream, unable to get the addict even a tiny bit stoned. The main obstacle to Naltrexone treatment is the addict himself. Very few people agree to take it, and of those that do, many drop-out early from treatment (Fram *et al*, 1989). It works far too well for its own good and most heroin addict's liking.There have been claims that it can block alcohol from having any effect as well, but I have met people who have taken Naltrexone and still been able to get as drunk as they like.

Where Naltrexone proves useful is as a form of safety net after treatment for addiction. This can mean that the addict is still technically dependent on a drug (ie. Naltrexone), but it's not one that's going to make him believe that it makes more sense to watch Riki Lake than to get dressed or eat.

There are other drugs that are used to restrain heroin addiction. Buprenorphine is the best of the rest. It has the curious property of getting the user slightly stoned, but blocking other opiates that do the same (eg. heroin). It comes in small tablets and can be fiddly to use, but it's quite a useful drug if you've got a heroin habit that you don't particularly want.

Family therapy

This is still a relatively unusual form of treatment for addiction, which is strange, as few of us live in total isolation. We are surrounded to a greater or lesser extent by a network of friends and relations. Some of these relationships are of real value to an addicted client, and continue to be so once he has cut down or given up altogether.

Different family therapists have differing thoughts on addiction. Some believe that the addict clearly has a life-threatening problem, and it's the job of the therapist to make everyone as supportive as possible to ensure the addict or alcoholic the best possible chance of success. No easy job when you come to consider how hurt many family members may have been by living in the epicentre of chemical mayhem.

On the far side of the spectrum are the family therapists who describe the addict or the alcoholic as the 'identified patient'. You can read into that what you like, but it sounds like there's an assumption that the whole family is not too well, but only one member is showing the symptoms.

The whole family, excluding younger children, are usually invited to attend a meeting, and everyone sits in a circle with one or perhaps two therapists. Family therapy can be a very technical activity, and there might be CCTV cameras and microphones in the room, and a separate control room where even more therapists are sitting, watching the television and listening to what is being said. At some point they might communicate with the therapist sitting with the family and suggest things like, 'Ask them what the children do when mum and dad start fighting'. This allows things that would otherwise never be mentioned to be discussed.

Depending on their training and natural way of working, some family therapists will form a closer bond with one or more members of the family. The thinking here is that the family is out of balance, and by putting his or her weight behind particular individuals, a shift can occur in the way the family sets about the business of getting on. Other therapists may remain very impartial, encouraging family members to talk to one another rather than via the professional. Family therapy can be baffling, with the therapist asking one member of the family what they suppose another member of the family might feel about a third member of the family. Or the therapist may ask someone not to speak at all, but instead to mime how they feel. There's even weirder stuff than this, involving conversations with empty chairs, or everyone becoming statues. Sometimes it's as if the therapists themselves are on drugs. Alongside these apparently daft parlour games, family therapists will set homework for the family. Good practical assignments like, 'Go out as a family to somewhere new at the weekend', or, 'Buy each of yourselves a treat'.

Family therapists are a strange breed. They can't even keep from meddling with something as practical as this. They might suggest, for instance, that the family spend two days without talking to one another, or that dad should go out even earlier to the pub. The thinking here is that many families say that they can't change, but with the help of a friendly family therapist they soon learn that they can change – they can get worse!

Family therapy is probably not the number one tool for fixing addiction. It only takes one or two key relations to withdraw from the meetings for the therapy to finish before it can get anywhere. It can also let addiction off the hook a bit by tracking down any number of interesting but irrelevant family red herrings. It is, however, a good method for shaking the tree, making change a possibility. There's also evidence that where family therapy is bolted onto the individual treatment of an addict or alcoholic, that 'patient' tends to drink less or use fewer drugs than a similar client who did not receive family therapy (Georgiakis, 1995; Clerici *et al*, 1988).

Religion

Turning to God for salvation has been an almost constant theme in addiction for the past two hundred years. Armchair mystics and pub philosophers swell the ranks of the brotherhood of addiction. Shifting levels of consciousness mean that, for the earlier part of the evening at least, the drug-altered mind can see things from a different and perhaps deeper perspective. Many shamanist cultures have based their religious ceremonies on hallucinogenic plants and fungi.

Maybe a component of addiction could be the yearning for profound or spiritual experience. There certainly seems to be a tie-in between addiction and religion. It might be a matter of conversion from one form of conscious raising to another, or the necessity for a cure that's as powerful as the sickness. If you're not religious yourself it can feel uncomfortable to see a grizzled cynical street addict turn into a meek and gentle lamb of God. The thought may occur, 'Well if they could brainwash him, none of us are safe'. But maybe he's just trying out another paradise. The more traditional one.

One of the major attractions of accepting religious help has to be the Christian tradition of repentance and forgiveness. The addict has done wrong by most people's judgement, but the teachings of Christ mean that he is welcomed rather than condemned. He is the embodiment of the parable of the prodigal son. Further reason to enter a religious community is the appeal of order after chaos, calm in place of lunacy, and sanctuary to end danger.

A common destination for addicts is the lost land of serenity. The more chemicals they use to attain some peace of mind, the further they seem to drift from it. Religious communities are tranquil places as a rule, and like the mind of an active addict, they are removed from the day-to-day world. So again, two worlds that couldn't be further apart – that of the frantic urban drug addict, and a cloistered disciplined community – turn out to have much in common.

The oddly spiritual complexion to addiction comes out in Alcoholics Anonymous philosophy too, with its belief in the possibility of 'spiritual re-awakening'. Something finer does go to sleep once addiction takes hold. The addict now laughs less and less, perhaps because they've traded repetitive chemistry for spontaneous joy. They've become all science and no art. The true self, if we have such a thing, can't get much of a look-in. It probably gives up, figuratively speaking. Hope fades away with this addict's true or core self, and from this point on he or she is in big trouble.

The addict has now lost a part of him or herself. Each day brings a sense of dread as if something bad is about to happen, but they can't say what. There's also a feeling of emptiness, or nothingness even. The drugs have stopped working. He or she can't sleep. They look completely out of it, but their mind is ticking away. So, too, is their life. They're not depressed as such – it's more a case of being dangerously dispirited. Realising that things cannot possibly get any worse, they go and get help.

Addiction is now on the back foot, and it goes into hiding. It can wait. It gets an early chance to re-emerge if temptation comes the addict's way, even though he or she doesn't want any more drink or drugs. It's another of addiction's paradoxes that the addict will go to tremendous lengths to avoid a drug, then show almost no resistance to it should it be offered on a strictly no-obligation basis.

The next opportunity comes when health returns. If we feel better and look better, we can reasonably assume that we are better. But if you have a proper copper-bottomed addiction, looking and feeling better mean nothing at all, other than you're ready to get out there and get nicely trashed. And the addict knows this. They've been around long enough to learn that some clean time reduces their tolerance to drugs, making their effect that much stronger and therefore more offending.

And there's the boredom factor as well. Tranquillity, serenity, humility, cup of tea; it's all very nice, but where's the thrill? Evangelical Christianity, sometimes derisively called 'Happy Clappy' worship, can deliver more of a high than most churches, but the devil has the better tunes. Somewhere in the city Lou Reed (*Heroin*, 1967) is singing:

> *Heroin,*
> *It's my wife,*
> *And it's my life.*

Time to go. But, some people don't go – or go back that is. They dare to move into a new and scary drug-free life and, scarier still, find out more about themselves. They haven't been too curious before, as people have had largely critical observations to make. They wanted to be out of their heads, not in them.

With a global network of churches, the chance to wipe the slate clean and be born again, and an enviable record on non-judgement (inquisitions and witch-hunts exempted), a religious community represents a real possibility for recovery.

Group therapy

At this stage we can probably agree that someone with a serious addiction problem will find it difficult to give up without help. An obvious answer, and one which alcoholics have been using by instinct for over 160 years, is to get together with other addicts and form a self-help group or mutual aid society (White, 1999). Individual members can then support one another by offering sympathy and by acting as one another's mental policeman, blowing a whistle whenever they notice the tell-tale signs of addictive thinking or actions creeping into the ways of a fellow member. These benefits have been turned into a practical system of working by the introduction of a counsellor. What we then have is something optimistically known as group therapy.

Group therapy features a counsellor or two, approximately six to ten addicts, and some awkward silences. Eventually someone can study the pattern of the carpet no longer, and they'll start talking. Things start happening from there.

Perhaps because they are generally sociable people, addicts and alcoholics seem to respond well to what's generally called group therapy. It's not for everyone. As with AA or NA meetings, there's always a risk that someone may feel excluded. They may be of the wrong sex, the wrong social background, the wrong race, or have a real gift for annoying other people. They may also suffer from social anxiety, ie. the fear of groups. So group therapy cannot be expected to be good for all.

One of the important ways in which groups can help an addict is by offering him or her acceptance. This is significant because addiction is an activity that says that the normal state – sober/straight – is unacceptable. To go one step further, addiction might be saying that the true, chemical-free person underneath this smokescreen, is unacceptable. After a few years of being thoroughly objectionable to a number of people he or she really cares about, the addict may have good reason to judge him or herself unacceptable. Robbery, deception, assault, prostitution, misuse and neglect of loved ones, they're all possible once you enter the crazy kingdom of addiction. If you weren't too impressed by yourself when you went in, you are definitely going to feel less than proud after this sort of misbehaviour.

To avoid the guilt and shame that will crowd into your mind with the sober light of day, there's always more of your chosen anaesthetic: or, the group. It can be almost as hard to forgive ourselves for things we've done to other people as it can be to forgive other people for things they've done to us. But, it's far easier to forgive people for things they did to someone else. Are you still with me? Now, if an addict were to then ask virtual strangers for their verdicts on the regrettable things that he or she has been up to, it's possible that these strangers (ie. the other members of the group), will show some understanding, and not judge the addict too harshly. They realise that they haven't exactly qualified for a Nobel peace prize themselves lately, and the topic of addicts behaving badly can stir them into telling some grim tales of their own. By a system of reciprocal confession from each of its members, the group can mutually forgive each other for being so inconsiderate to other people.

But what about people who are in the room? According to Irvine Yalom (1991), if some of the group don't treat each other so well, this should be seen as an opportunity rather than a problem. If a row breaks out between individual members of the group, they should be helped to understand what it is about one another that they dislike. This is supposed to be positive in a funny kind of way, because it may highlight problems that the respective arguers have had in generally getting along with other people. If the group therapist can help all present to come up with their angle on things, an objective view can be formed which makes it apparent to the warring parties that they both had a part to play in the conflict. Both members can then go away and ruminate on what's been said, or 'sulk' as it's generally known.

The hope is that they'll work out a better future way to deal with people they have some trouble sticking. One of the arguers may, for instance, think twice before interrupting someone else. The other group member might have learnt that it's better to speak up sooner when he's unhappy, rather than bottling it up then suddenly exploding with anger. Skilfully handled, this method of therapy via peacemaking can be very impressive. Whether it helps people to give up drugs or not is far less certain, but powerful negative feelings such as anger and resentment have frequently been identified as the cause of addicts going back to the bottle or the syringe. There's a chance that a new angle on how to avoid unnecessary conflict can reduce one area where negative feelings might flourish.

Groups are useful on a number of levels. They offer a powerful experience – something addicts find irresistible as a rule. Its members often appreciate the intensity of an intimate group. Moreover, the secrets of others are always intriguing. Eight heads are better than one, and a group can be used to offer solutions to life problems such as relationship mending, or returning to work or home. As I've already mentioned, negative emotions are a major factor in many relapses. A group is an environment where people can 'spill out' their frustration or upset, and so be less burdened by feelings that are risky to carry around town.

It's human to forget the bad times. Perhaps this is a natural trait which stops us becoming too pessimistic and depressed about life ahead. This tendency to forget pain is probably, therefore, helpful, except when it comes to something like addiction. Six months – or six weeks, even (Jenkins *et al*, 1979) – of clean and sober time and the memories begin to fade. Domestic strife, severe sickness, beatings from drug creditors, arrests, the sack, they can all melt away. By hearing other people tell their stories of addiction grief, an alcoholic or addict has similar memories stirred up. These 'sobering' recollections can increase an addict's concern – and therefore his vigilance – towards drink and drugs. With addiction, you need to be on the lookout.

Final note

The Englishman often mistakes a fact for the truth.

Oscar Wilde, 1890

You need to be careful with research. Interviewees sometimes lie and so too can researchers (Boseley, 2000).

Charlie, a good friend of mine, was studying for a psychology degree, and as part of the course he had to come up with a piece of original research. He ran short on time and made up some of the characters and their answers at the last minute. A few months later Charlie was in a class where the lecturer was stating how valuable research was because it gave us the facts. Charlie stopped him at that point to say that research was easily faked and therefore couldn't be trusted. The lecturer would not accept this – academics were honourable scientists and their work was thoroughly scrutinised. 'Of course research is made up. I made up my research for this course', said Charlie, in a moment of student suicide. The lecturer now had a dilemma: should he believe Charlie, in which case he'd lose the argument and with it his faith in the integrity of research; or should he deny Charlie's confession, win the argument and let my friend off the hook? He took the second option. Charlie got his degree, but he never practised psychology. That one conversation probably taught him all he really needed to know about the subject.

Another point to consider when reading facts and figures gathered from addicts is that they often come from people who have gone to see a doctor or nurse for help with their chemical intake. Most members of the public don't do this. In fact, most alcoholics and drug addicts don't. A great deal of what we think we know about addiction is based on the study of a small proportion of addicts, and this sub-group tends to have a more severe form of addiction (Robson and Bruce, 1997). Research costs money, and the 'facts' they uncover can depend on who the paymaster is. Turner and Spilich (1997), for instance, found that researchers who had been sponsored by the tobacco industry were likely to 'discover' that nicotine makes our brains work better.

Drug addiction research is still in its infancy. There's far more known about alcoholism, so I've had to tip this book in the direction of alcohol research. In ten years time, when much more is known about the nature of drug addiction, a much more balanced account should be possible.

This relates to my final caution, which is the danger of generalisation. The life experience of a group of middle-aged white alcoholics from a small American town in the mid-1950s bears little resemblance to the world of a young female crack addict living in London at the start of the twenty-first century.

It's easy to back a point up by finding a piece of research that supports your view. It should not be forgotten, though, that in some journal somewhere there's an equally valid piece of work that produces evidence that directly contradicts such opinions. I've tried to be unbiased, but I haven't dedicated my life to this end.

References

Abbott PJ, Weller SB, Delaney HD, Moore BA (1998) Community reinforcement approach in the treatment of opiate addicts. *Am J Drug Alcohol Abuse* **24**(1): 17–30

Abraham K (1908) The psychological relation between sexuality and alcoholism. In: Jones E (ed) (1960) *Selected Papers of Karl Abraham*. Basic Books, New York

Anderson DJ (1981) *Perspectives of Treatment. The Minnesota Experience*. Hazelden Books, Minnesota

Anglin MD, Kao C, Harlow LL, Peters K, Booth MW (1987) Similarity of behaviour with addict couples. Part I. Methodology and narcotics patterns. *Int J Addict* **22**(6): 497–524

Azrin N (1976) Improvements in the community-reinforcement approach to alcoholism. *Behaviour Res Thera*p **14**: 339–48

Bateson G (1956) Towards a theory of schizophrenia. *Behav Sci* **1**: 251

Bean MH (1975) Alcoholics Anonymous. *Psych Ann* **5**(2): 3–64

Becker JT, Jaffe JH (1984) Impaired memory for treatment relevant information. *J Stud Alcohol* **45**: 339–43

Beckman JJ (1975) Women Alcoholics. *J Stud Alcohol* **36**: 747

Begleiter H, Porjesz B, Bihari B, Kissin B (1984) Event-related brain potentials in boys at risk for alcoholism. *Science* **227**: 1493–1496

Beletsis S, Brown S (1981) A developmental framework for understanding the adult children of alcoholics. Focus on women. *J Addict Health* **2**: 187–203

Bell R, Wechsler H, Johnston LD (1997) Correlates of college student marijuana use: Results of a US national survey. *Addiction* **92**(5): 571–81

Benabud A (1957) Psychopathological aspects of the cannabis situation in Morroco: Statistical data for 1956. *Bull Narcotics* **9**: 2

Benowitz NL (1988) Toxicity of nicotine: Implications with regard to nicotine replacement therapy. In: Pomerlau CS (ed) *Nicotine Replacement: a Critical Evaluation*. Alan R Liss Publications, New York: 187–217

Besançon F (1993) Time to alcohol dependence after abstinence and first drink. *Addiction* **88**(12): 1647–50

The Bible, *Book of Genesis*, Chapter 3.7

Bickel WK, Marion I, Lowinson J (1987) The treatment of alcoholic methadone patients: A review. *J Subst Abuse Treatment* **4**: 15–19

Blum K, Noble EP, Sheridan PJ (1990) Allelic association of human D2 receptor gene in alcoholism. *J Am Med Assoc* **263**(15): 2055–60

Blume (1992) Alcohol and drug problems in women. In: Lowinsin JH, Ruiz P, Millman RB (eds) *Substance Abuse: a comprehensive textbook*. Williams and Wilkins, Baltimore, MD

Boseley S (2000) Doctors, 'Faking research work'. *The Guardian* 13 December, 2000

Bradshaw J (1997) *Creating Love: The Next Great Stage of Growth*. Piatkus, New York

Brady KT, Grice DE, Dunstan L, Randall C (1993) Gender differences in substance use disorders. *Am J Psychiatry* **150**(11): 1707–11

Breslau N, Fenn N, Peterson E (1993) Early smoking initiation and nicotine dependence in a cohort of young adults. *Drug Alcohol Depend* **33**(2): 129–37

Brooks JE (1953) *The Mighty Leaf*. Barnard and Westwood, London

Buckroyd J (1996) *Eating your heart out: understanding and overcoming eating disorders*. Trafalgar Square, London

Bureau of Narcotics (1930) *Presentment and Report by the Grand Jury on the Subject of Narcotic Traffic*. Bureau of Narcotics: 19 Feb

Burroughs W (1954) *Junky*. Penguin Books Ltd, Harmondsworth

Byrne DG, Byrne AE, Reinhart MI (1993) Psychosocial correlates of adolescent cigarette smoking: Personality or environment? *Aust J Psychol* **45**(2): 87–95

Cabaj R (1992) Substance abuse in the gay and lesbian community. In: Lowinson J, Ruiz P, Millman R (eds) *Substance Abuse: a comprehensive textbook*. Williams and Wilkins, Baltimore, MD

Carnes P (1991) *Don't Call It Love, Recovery From Sexual Addiction*. Bantam Books, New York

Catalano R, Howard M, Hawkins J, Wells E (1988) Relapse in the addictions: rates, determinants, and promising prevention strategies. In: *1988 Surgeon General's Report on Health Consequences of Smoking*. US Government Printing Office, Washington

Childress AR, Ehrman R, McLellan AT, O'Brien CP (1988) Conditioned craving and arousal in cocaine addiction: A preliminary report. In: Problems of Drug Dependence. *NIDA Res Monograph* **81**: 74–80

Childress AR, Ehrman R, Rohsenow DJ et al (eds) (1992) Classically conditioned factors in drug dependence. In: *Substance Abuse: a comprehensive textbook*. Williams and Wilkins, Baltimore, MD

Chopra RN, Chopra GS (1939) The recent position of hemp. Drug addiction in India. *Indian Med Res Mem*: 31

Christo G (1998) A review of reasons for using or not using drugs: commonalities between sociological and clinical perspectives. *Drugs: Education, Prevention and Policy* **5**(1): 59–72

Clerici J, Garini R, Capitanio C, Zardi L, Carta I, Gori E (1988) Involvement of families in group therapy of heroin addicts. *Drug Alcohol Depend* **21**(3): 213–16

Cloninger CR (1987) Neurogenetic adaptive mechanisms in alcoholism. *Science* **236**: 410–16

Cochrane C, Malcolm R, Brewerton T (1998) The role of weight control as a motivation for cocaine abuse. *Addictive Behaviours* **23**(2): 201–7

Cole-Harding S, Wilson JR (1987) Ethanol Metabolism in Men and Women. *J Stud Alcohol* **48**: 380–7

Collison M (1996) In search of the high life: Drugs, crime masculinities and consumption. *Br J Criminology* **36**(3): 428–44

Comings DE, Muhleman D, Ahn C, Gysin R, Flanagan SD (1994) The dopamine D2 receptor gene: A genetic risk factor in substance misuse. *Drug Alc Dependence* **34**(3): 175–80

Corkery JM (1997) *Statistics of Drug Addicts Notified to the Home Office, United Kingdom, 1996.* Government Statistical Service

Corrigan EM (1980) *Alcoholic Women in Treatment.* Oxford University Press, Oxford

Covitz JD (1986) *Emotional Child Abuse: The family curse.* Sigo Press, US

Crundall IA (1993) Correlates of student substance abuse. *Drug Alcohol Rev* **12**(3): 271–6

Cutten GB (1908) *The Psychology of Alcoholism.* Scott Publishing, New York

Dackis CA, Gold MS (1992) Psychiatric hospitals for treatment of dual diagnosis. In: Daley DC, Marlatt GA (1992) Relapse Prevention: Cognitive and Behavioural Interventions. In: Lowinsin JH, Ruiz P, Millman RB (eds) *Substance Abuse: a comprehensive textbook.* Williams and Wilkins, Baltimore, MD

Daley DC, Marlatt GA (1992) Relapse prevention: cognitive and behavioral interventions. In: Lowinson JH, Ruiz P, Millman RB, Langrod JG (eds) *Substance Abuse: a comprehensive textbook.* Williams and Wilkins, Baltimore, MD: 533–42

Darke S (1994) The use of benzodiazepines among injecting drug users. *Drug Alcohol Rev* **13**(1): 63–69

Davies JB, Baker R (1987) The impact of self-presentation and interviewer bias effects on self-reported heroin use. *Br J Addiction* **82**: 907–12

Davies JB (1997) *The Myth of Addiction.* Harwood Academic Publishers, Amsterdam

Davoli M, Perucci CA, Rapiti E, Bargagli AM, D'Ippoliti D, Forastiere F, Abeni D (1997) A persistent rise in mortality among injection drug users in Rome, 1980 through 1992. *Am J Public Health* **87**(5): 851–3

Dawson DA (1998) Alcohol, drugs and suicide attempt/ideation. *Addiction Res* **5**(6): 451–72

de la Fluente L, Barrio G, Royuela L, Braco MJ (1997) The transition from injecting to smoking heroin in three Spanish cities. *Addiction* **92**(12): 1479–63

DeLeon G, Wexler HK, Janchill N (1982) The therapeutic community: success and improvement rate five years after treatment. *Int J Addict* **17**: 703–47

DeLint J, Schmidt W (1971) *The Epidemiology of Alcoholism. Biological Basis of Alcoholism*. Wiley-Interscience Pubs, New York

Del Pozo L, Gomez CF, Fraile MG, Perez IV (1998) Psychological and behavioural factors associated with relapse among heroin abusers treated in therapeutic communities. *Addictive Behaviours* **23**(2): 155–69

Drake RE, Vaillant GE (1988) Predicting alcoholism and personality disorder in a 33-year longitudinal study of children of alcoholics. *Br J Addiction* **83**: 799–807

Drugscope (2000) *Barbiturate Database.* www.drugscope.org.uk 16.07.2000.

Edmunds M, May T, Hearnden I, Hough M (1998) *Arrest referral: emerging lessons from research. Drugs Prevention Initiative*. Paper 23. HMSO, London

Edwards G, Gross MM (1976) Alcohol dependence: provisional description of a clinical syndrome. *Br Med J* **1**: 1058–1061

Edwards G, Orford J (1977) Alcoholism: A controlled trial of 'treatment' and 'advice'. *J Stud Alcohol* **38**: 1004–31

Edwards G, Brown D, Duckitt A, Oppenheimer E, Sheehan M, Taylor C (1987) Outcome of alcoholism: the structure of patient attributions as to what causes change. *Br J Addict* **82**: 533–45

Edwards G, Marshall EJ, Cook CC (1997) *The Treatment of Drinking Problems*. CUP, Cambridge

Ehrman R, Ternes J, O'Brien CP, McLellan AT (1992), Conditioned tolerance in human opiate addicts. *Psychopharmacol* **108**: 1–2, 218–24

Emrick C (1974) A review of psychologically oriented treatment of alcoholism. *J Stud Alcohol* **35**: 523–49

Emrick CD (1987) Alcoholics Anonymous affiliation process and effectiveness as treatment. *Alcohol Clin Exp Res* **11**: 416–23

Escobedo LG, Peddicord JP (1997) Long-term trends in cigarette smoking among young US adults. *Addictive Behaviours* **22**(3): 427–30

European Monitoring Centre for Drugs and Drug Addiction (2000) *Annual report on the state of the drugs problem in the European Union*. EMCDDA, Luxembourg

Fals-Stewart W, Birchler GR, Ellis L (1999) Procedures for evaluating the dyadic adjustment of drug-abusing patients and their intimate partners: a multimethod assessment approach. *J Subst Abuse Treat* **16**(1): 5–16

Farrell M, Ward J, Mattick R, Hall W, Stimson GV, des Jarlais D *et al* (1994) Methadone maintenance: A review. *Br Med J* **38**: 997–1001

Farrell M (1995) *A review of the legislation, regulation and delivery of methadone in 12 member states of the European Union*. Office of the Official Publications of the European Union, Luxembourg

References

Flint AJ, Novotny TE (1997) Poverty status and cigarette smoking prevalence and cessation in the United States, 1983–1993: The independent risk of being poor. *Tobacco Control* **6**(1): 14–18

Finney JW, Moos RH (1981) Characteristics and prognoses of alcoholics who become moderate drinkers and abstainers after treatment. *J Stud Alcohol* **42**: 94–105

Fishbein DH, Jaffe JH, Snyder FR, Haertzen CA, Hickey JE (1993) Drug users' self-reports of behaviors and affective states under the influence of alcohol. *Int J Addict* **28**(14): 1565–85

Fossey E (1993) Identification of alcohol by smell among young children: an objective measure of early learning in the home. *Drug and Alcohol Dep* **34**(1): 29–35

Fram DH, Marmo J, Holden R (1989) Naltrexone treatment – the problem of patient acceptance. *J Subst Abuse Treatment* **6**: 119–122

Frankenstein W, Hay WM, Nathan PE (1985) Effects of intoxication on alcoholics' marital communications and problem-solving. *J Stud Alcohol* **46**(1): 1–6

Freud S (1884) Uber Coca. In: Byck R (ed) *Cocaine Papers, 1974.* Stonehill Publishing: 49–73

Freud S (1985) *The Complete Letters of Sigmund Freud to Wilhelm Fliess.* Harvard University Press: 287

Frezza M, Di Padoua C, Pozzato G *et al* (1990) High blood alcohol levels in women: the role of decreased gastric alcohol dehydrogenase and first-pass metabolism. *New Eng J Med* **322**: 95–9

Galanter M, Castaneda R, Salamon I (1987) Institutional self-help therapy for alcoholism: clinical outcome. *Alcoholism: Clin Exper Res* **11**: 424–29

Gavaler JS (1982) Sex-related differences in ethanol-induced liver disease: artifactual or real? *Alcohol, Clin Exp Res* **6**: 186–196

Gawin FH, Ellinwood EH (1988) Cocaine and other stimulants. *New Eng J Med* **318**:1173

Georgakis A (1995) *Evaluation of a Residential Alcohol and Drug Dependency Treatment Centre.* Clouds Publications, Salisbury

Georgiakis A (2000) Personal correspondence

Gfroerer JC, Brodsky MD (1993) Frequent cocaine users and their use of treatment. *Amer J Public Health* **83**(8): 1149–54

Glassner B, Berg B (1980) How Jews Avoid Alcohol Problems. *Am Sociol Rev* **45**: 647–64

Glatt M (1982) Reflections on the Treatment of Alcoholism in Women. *Brit J Alcohol* **14**(2): 77–83

Goehl L, Nunes E, Quitkin F, Hilton I (1993) Social networks and methadone treatment outcome: the costs and benefits of social ties. *Am J Drug Alcohol Abuse* **19**(3): 251–62

Goodwin DW (1979) Alcoholism and heredity. *Arch Gen Psychiatry* **36**: 57–61

Goodwin DW (1992) Alcohol: clinical aspects. In: Lowinsin JH, Ruiz P, Millman RB (eds) *Substance Abuse: a comprehensive textbook.* Williams and Wilkins, Baltimore, MD

Gorski T (1995) *Relapse Prevention Counselling Workbook: Managing High-Risk Situations.* Independence Press, New York

Greden JF, Procter A, Victor B (1981) Caffeinism associated with greater use of other psychotropic agents. *Compr Psychiatry* **22**: 565

Hagan TA (1987) *A retrospective search for the aetiology of drug abuse: a background comparison of a drug-addicted population of women.* NIDA Research Monograph, Health and Human Resources

Harris E, Barrowclough B (1997) Suicide as an outcome for mental disorder. *Br J Psychiatry* **170**: 205

Harrison L, Carr-Hill R, Sutton M (1993) Consumption and harm: drinking patterns of the Irish, the English and the Irish in England. *Alcohol Alcohol* **28**(6): 715–23

Harwood HJ, Hubbard RL, Collins JJ, Rachal JV (1988) The costs of crime and the benefits of drug abuse treatment: a cost-benefit analysis using TOPS data. *NIDA Research Monograph* **86**, US Dept of Health and Human Services, Washington DC

Hazan AR, Lipton HL, Glantz SA (1994) Popular films do not reflect current tobacco use. *Am J Pub Health* **84**(6): 998–1000

Heath AC, Jardine R, Martin NG (1989) Interactive effects of genotype and social environment on alcohol consumption in female twins. *J Study Alcohol* **50**: 38–48

Heath RG (1964) Pleasure Response of Human Beings to Direct Stimulation of the Brain: Physilogic and Psychodynamic Considerations. In: Heath RG (ed) *The Role of Pleasure in Behaviour.* Hoeber, New York: 219–243

Heather N, Robertson I (1997) *Problem Drinking.* Oxford Medical Publications, Oxford

Hillbom M, Holm L (1986) Contribution of Traumatic Head Injury to Neuropsychological Deficits in Alcoholics. *J Neurol Neurosurg Psychiatry* **49**: 1348–53

Home Office (1998) *Statistics of Deaths Reported to Coroners, England and Wales.* HMSO, London

Hope S, Power C, Rodgers B (1998) The relationship between parental separation in childhood and problem drinking in adulthood. *Addiction* **93**(4): 505–14

Høyer G, Nilssen O, Brenn T, Schirmer H (1994) Norwegians and cheap alcohol: consumption in a low price area. *Nordisk Alkoholtidskrift* **11**(3): 139–46

Hubbard RL (1992) Evaluation and Treatment Outcome. In : Lowinsin JH, Ruiz P, Millman RB (eds) *Substance Abuse: a comprehensive textbook.* Williams and Wilkins, Baltimore, MD

Huss M (1851) *Alcoholismus Chronicus eller Chronisk Alkohosjukdom,* 2 Vols. Out of print

References

Irwin M, Schuckit MA, Smith TL (1990) Clinical importance of age of onset in type 1 and type 2 primary alcoholics. *Arc Gen Psychiatry* **47**: 320–24

Jasinski DR, Johnson RE, Henningfield JE (1984) Abuse liability assessment in human subjects. *Trends Pharmacol Sci* **5**(5): 196–200

Jenkins CD, Hurst MW, Rose RM (1979) Life changes: do people really remember? *Arch Gen Psychiatry* **36**: 379–84

Jessor R, Donovan JE, Costa F (1990) Personality, Perceived Life Chances and Adolescent Behaviour. In: Hurrellman K, Losel F (eds) *Health Hazards in Adolescence*. Walter de Gruyter Publishing, New York

Johnson BD, Muffler J (1992) Sociocultural Aspects of Drug Use and Abuse in the 1990s. In: Lowinsin JH, Ruiz P, Millman RB (eds) *Substance Abuse: a comprehensive textbook*. Williams and Wilkins, Baltimore, MD

Joseph H, Appel P (1985) Alcoholism and methadone treatment: consequences for the patient and the programme. *Am J Drug Alcohol Issues* **11**(1&2): 37–53

Joseph MH, Young AM, Gray JA (1996) Are neurochemistry and reinforcement enough – can the abuse potential of drugs be explained by common actions on a dopamine reward system in the brain? *Hum Psychopharmacol* **11** (supplement): 55–63

Kaufman E (1976) The abuse of multiple drugs: psychological hypotheses, treatment considerations. *Am J Drug Alcohol Abuse* **3**: 293

Kaufman E (1992) Family Therapy: A Treatment Approach to Substance Abusers In: Lowinsin JH, Ruiz P, Millman RB (eds) *Substance Abuse: a comprehensive textbook*. Williams and Wilkins, Baltimore, MD

Keane TM, Wolfe J (1990) Co-morbidity in post-traumatic disorder: an analysis of community and clinical studies. *J Consult Clin Psychiatry* **50**: 138–140

Keller Phelps J, Nourse AE (1986) *The Hidden Addiction and How to Get Free*. Little Brown and Company, Boston, London

Kennedy O (1971) Pupillometrics as an aid in the assessment of motivation, impact of treatment, and prognosis of chronic alcoholics. *Dissertation Abstracts International* **32**(2-b): 1214–5

Kernberg O (1975) Treatment of narcassistic personality disorders, *Bulletin of the Menninger Clinic* **39**(5): 409–19

Khantzian EJ (1981) Some Treatment Implications of the Ego and Self Disturbances in Alcoholism. In: Bean MH, Zinberg NE (eds) *Dynamic Approaches to the Understanding and Treatment off Alcoholism*. MacMillan, Basingstoke:163–93

Khantzian EJ (1985) The self-medication hypothesis of addictive disorders: focus on heroin and cocaine dependence. *Am J Psychiatry* **142**: 1259–64

Killam KF, Olds J, Sinclair J (1957) Further Studies on the Effects of Centrally Acting Drugs on Self-Stimulation. *J Pharmacol Exp Ther* **119**: 157

Kirkpatrick J (1978) *Turnabout: New Help for the Woman Alcoholic.* Doubleday, New York

Knight RP (1937) The dynamics and treatment of chronic alcohol addiction. *Bulletin of the Menninger Clinic* **1**: 233–50

Kutz E (1979) *Not-God: A History of Alcoholics Anonymous.* Hazelden Books, Center City, Minnesota

Kraepelin E (1883) *Compendium of Psychiatry*

Laberg JC, Ellersten B (1987) Psychophysiological indications of craving in alcoholics: effects of cue exposure. *Br J Addict* **82**: 1341–48

Latkin CA, Mandell W (1993) Depression as an antecedent of frequency of intravenous drug use in an urban, non-treatment sample. *Int J Addictions* **28**(14): 1601–12

Lex BW, Lukas SE, Greenwald NE, Mendelson JH (1988) Alcohol-induced changes in body sway in women at risk for alcoholism: a pilot study. *J Stud Alcohol* **49**: 346–50

Li HZ, Rosenblood L (1994) Exploring factors influencing alcohol consumption patterns among Chinese and Caucasians. *J Stud Alcohol* **55**(4): 427–33

Lindberg S, Agren G (1988) Mortality among male and female hospitalized alcoholics in Stockholm 1962–1983. *Br J Addiction* **83**: 1193–200.

Linstrom L (1992) *Managing Alcoholism: Matching Clients to Treatments.* Oxford University Press, Oxford

Little R, Clontz K (1994) Young, drunk, dangerous and driving: underage drinking and driving research findings. *J Alcohol Drug Educ* **39**(2): 37–49

Lowinger P (1977) The solution to narcotic addiction in the People's Republic of China. *Am J Drug Alcohol Abuse* **4**: 165

McCarty D, Morrison S, Mills KC (1983) Attitudes, beliefs and alcohol use. *J Stud Alcohol* **44**(2): 338

McGregor C, Darke S, Ali R, Christie P (1998) Experience of non-fatal overdose among heroin users in Adelaide, Australia: circumstances and risk perceptions. *Addiction* **93**(5): 701–11

McGue M, Slutske W, Taylor J, Iacono WG (1997) Personality and substance use disorders: effects of gender and alcoholism subtype. *Alcohol Clin Exper Res* **21**(3): 513–20

McLellan AT, Luborsky L, Erdlen R, LaPorte DJ, Intintolo V (1980) The addiction severity index. In: Gottheil AYT, McLellan AT, Druley K (eds) *A Substance Misuse and Psychiatric Illness.* Pergamon Press, New York: 151–59

McMahon J, Jones BT (1993) Negative expectancy in motivation. *Addiction Res* **1**(2): 145–155

McQueen Z (2000) Personal correspondence

Magura S, Siddiqi Q, Freeman R, Lipton DS (1991) *Changes in Cocaine Use After Entry to Methadone Treatment.* Narcotic and Drug Research Inc, New York

Makela P (1998) Alcohol-related mortality by age and sex and its impact on the Finnish Death Register. *Eur J Public Health* **8**(1): 43–51

Marks J (1996) Acidy, addiction and the prohibition. *Addiction Res* **4**(2): i–v

Marks J (1997) Personal correspondence

Marlatt GA, Demming B, Reid JB (1973) Loss of control drinking in alcoholics: an experimental analogue. *J Abnormal Psychology* **81**: 233–41

Marlatt GA (1978) Craving for Alcohol, Loss of Control and Relapse: Cognitive-Behavioural Analysis. In: Nathan PE, Marlatt GA, Loberg T (eds) *Alcoholism: New Directions in Behavioural Research and Treatment.* Plenum Press, New York

Marlatt GA, Gordon JR (1985) *Relapse Prevention: Maintenance Strategies in the Treatment of Addictive Behaviours.* Guildford Press, Guildford

Martin CS, Arria AM, Mezzich AC, Bukstein OG (1993) Patterns of polydrug use in adolescent alcohol abusers. *Am J Drug Alcohol Abuse* **19**(4): 511–21

Martin WR, Jasinski DR (1969) Physical parameters of morphine dependence in man: tolerance, early abstinence, protracted abstinence. *J Psychiatric Res* **7**: 9–17

Martin WR, Jasinski DR, Haertzen CA (1973) Methadone – a re-evaluation. *Arch Gen Psychiatry* **28**: 286–295

Marzuk PM, Tardiff K, Leon AC, Stajic M, Morgan EB, Mann JJ (1990) Prevalence of recent cocaine use among motor vehicle fatalities in new york city. *JAMA* **263**: 250–6

Mayer J, Price DO, Rafii A (1977) Antagonism of acupuncture analgesia in man by the narcotic naloxone. *Brain Res* **121**: 368–72

Miller BA, Downs WR, Gonodoli DM, Keil A (1987) The role of childhood sexual abuse in the development of alcoholism in women. *Violence Victims* **2**: 157–72

Miller NS, Gold MS (1989) Cocaine: general characteristics, abuse and addiction. *NY State J Med* **89**: 390–95

Miller NS, Belkin BM, Gold MS (1990) Multiple addictions: cosynchronous use of alcohol and drugs. *NY State J Med.* **90**: 596–600

Miller WR, Hester RK (1986) The Effectiveness of Alcoholism Treatment. What Research Reveals. In: Heather N, Miller WR (eds) *Treating Addictive Behaviours: Processes of Change.* Plenum Books, New York

Mills JK, Sirgo VI, Hartjes DT (1993) Perceptions of excessive alcohol consumption in stressful and non-stressful situations among undergraduates. *J Psychol* **127**(5): 543–6

Minuchin S (1975) *Families and Family Therapy*. Harvard University Press, Cambridge MA

Moncrieff J, Drummond DC, Candy B, Checinski K, Farmer R (1996) Sexual abuse in people with alcohol problems: a study of the prevalence of sexual abuse and its relationship to drinking behaviour. *Br J Psychiatry* **169**(3): 355–60

Morgan JP (1982) The Jamaica Ginger Paralysis. *JAMA* **248**: 1864–7

Morse GR (1999) *Detoxification*. Quay Books, Mark Allen Publishing Ltd, Salisbury

Mueller T, Lavori P, Keller M, Swortz A, Warshaw M, Hosin D *et al* (1994) Prognostic Effect of the Variable Course of Alcoholism on the 10-Year Course of Depression. *Am J Psychiatry* **151**(5): 701–6

Nakken C (1996) *The Addictive Personality*. Hazelden Books, Center City, Minnesota

Naranjo CA, Sellers EM, Sullivan JT *et al* (1987) The serotonin uptake inhibitor citaprolam attenuates ethanol in-take. *Clin Pharmacol Ther* **41**: 266–274

Narayan KM, Chadha SL, Hanson RL, Tandon R, Shekhawat S, Fernandes RJ, Gopinath N (1996) Prevalence and patterns of smoking in Delhi: cross sectional study. *Br Med J* **312**(7046): 1576–79

Narcotics Anonymous (1988) *Narcotics Anonymous*. 5th edn. Narcotic Anonymous World Services Inc, Location

National Institute of Drug Abuse (1989) Cocaine Use. In: *Monitoring the Future Study*. NIDA, Rockville, MD

National Institute on Drug Abuse, Capsules (1990) *Substance Abuse Among Blacks in the US*. NIDA, Rockville, MD: February

National Treatment Outcomes Research Study (1999) NTORS: Two year outcomes. Changes in substance use. *Health and Crime*, 4th Bulletin, Dept of Health Publications, London

Neumark YD, Anthony JC (1997) Childhood misbehaviour and the risk of injecting drug use. *Drug and Alcohol Dep* **48**(3): 193–97

Niaura RS, Rohsenow DJ, Binkoff JA, Monti P (1989) Responses to smoking-related stimuli and early relapse to smoking. *Addict Behaviour* **14**: 419–428

Nichter M, Nichter M, Vuckovic W, Quintero G, Ritenbaugh C *et al* (1997) Smoking, experimentation and initiation among adolescent girls: qualitative and quantitative findings. *Tobacco Control* **6**(4): 285–95

Ockene JG, Chiriboga DE, Zevallos JC (1996) Smoking in Equador: prevalence, knowledge and attitudes. *Tobacco Control* **5**(2): 121–6

O'Doherty M, Farrington A (1997) Estimating local opioid addict mortality. *Addiction Res* **4**(4): 321–7

Okazaki N, Fujita S, Suzuki K (1994) Comparative study of health problems between wives of alcoholics and control wives. *Japanese J Alcohol Studies Drug Dep* **29**(1): 23–30

Okruhlica L (1997) Epidemic of heroin use in slovakia. *Eur Addiction Res* **3**(2): 83–86

Olafsdottir H (1997) The dynamics of shifts in alcoholic beverage preference: effects of the legalization of beer in Iceland. *J Studies Alcohol* **59**(1): 107–14

Olson RP, Ganley R, Devine VT, Dorsey GC (1981) Long-term effects of behavioural versus insight-orientated therapy with inpatient alcoholics. *J Cons Clin Psychology* **49**: 866–877

OPCS (1996a) *Living in Britain: Results from the 1994 General Household Survey*. HMSO, London

OPCS (1996b) *Deaths registered in 1997 by cause and area of residence*. HMSO, London

Orbach S (1998) *Fat is a Feminist Issue*. Arrow Books, London

Orford J (2000) *Excessive Appetites: A psychological view of addictions*. John Wiley and Sons, London

Orford J, Edwards G (1977) *Alcoholism*. OUP, Oxford

Pear R (1990) United States reports poverty is down but inequality is up: report of the Census Bureau. *NY Times*, 26 September 1990

Pettinati HM, Sugerman AA, DiDonato N, Maurer HS (1982) The natural history of alcoholism over four years after treatment. *J Stud Alcohol* **43**: 201–15

Phelps J, Nourse AE (1986) *The Hidden Addiction and How to Get Free*. Little Brown and Co, Boston

Pierce JP, Gilpin E, Cavin SW (1997) Adult smokers who do not smoke daily. *Addiction* **92**(4): 473–80

Pine F (1990) *Drive Ego, Object and Self: A Synthesis of Clinical Work*. Basic Books, New York

Pedersen N (1981) Twin Similiarity for Usage of Common Drugs. In: Gedda L, Parisi P, Nance W (eds) *Twin Research 3: Epidemiological and Clinical Studies*. Alan R Liss, New York

Pendery ML, Maltzman IM, West LJ (1982) Controlled drinking by alcoholics? New findings and a re-evaluation of a major affirmative study. *Science* **217**: 169–75

Post RM, Kotin J, Goodwin FR (1974) The effects of cocaine on depressed patients. *Am J Psychiatry* **114**: 165–70

Pursch JA (1978) Physicians' Attitudinal Changes in Alcoholism. *Alcohol Clin Exper Rev* **2**(4): 358–61

Rausch JL, Monteiro MG, Schuckit MA (1991) Platelet serotonin uptake in men with family histories of alcoholism. *Neuropsychopharmacology* **4**: 83–6

Robins LN, Davis DH, Nurco DN (1974) How permanent was Vietnam drug addiction? *Am J Public Health* **64**: 38–43

Robson P, Bruce M (1997) A comparison of 'visible' and 'invisible' users of amphetamine, cocaine and heroin: Two distinct populations. *Addiction* **92**(12): 1729–36

Ross HE, Glaser FB, Stiasny S (1988) Sex differences in the prevalence of psychiatric disorder in patients with alcohol and drug problems. *Br J Addiction* **83**: 1179–92

Sanchez-Craig M, Walker K (1982) Teaching coping skills to alcoholics in a co-educational halfway house. *Br J Addiction* **77**: 35–50

Sanchez-Craig M, Wilkinson DA (1987) Treating problem drinkers who are not severely dependent on alcohol. *Drugs Soc* **1**(2/3): 39–67

Scher KJ (1983) Platelet monoamine oxidase activity in relatives of alcoholics. *Arch Gen Psychiatry* **39**: 137–40

Schmitz J, de Jong S, Roy A, Garnett D, Mosire V, Lamparski D *et al* (1993) Substance abuse among subjects screened out from an alcoholism research programme. *Am J Drug Alcohol Abuse* **19**(3): 359–68

Schuckit MA, Irwin M, Smith TL (1994) One-year incidence rate of major depression and other psychiatric disorders in 239 alcoholic men. *Addiction* **89**(4): 441–5

Schuckit MA, Klein J, Twitchell G, Smith T (1994a) Personality test scores as predictors of alcoholism almost a decade later. *Am J Psychiatry* **151**(7): 1038–42

Schuckit MA (1986) Genetic and clinical implications of alcoholism and affective disorder. *Am J Psychiatry* **143**: 140–7

Schuckit MA (1987) Biological vulnerability to alcoholism. *J Consult Clin Psychol* **55**: 301–9

Schuckit MA (1989) *Drug and Alcohol Abuse: A Clinical Guide to Diagnosis and Treatment*. Plenum Medical Book Co, New York

Schutte KK, Hearst J, Moos RH (1997) Gender differences in the relations between depressive symptoms and drinking behaviour among problem drinkers: a three-wave study. *J Consult Clin Psychology* **65**(3): 392–404

Sjoquist B, Eriksson A, Winblad B (1982) Salsolinol and Catecholamines in Human Brain and their Relation to Alcoholism. In: Bloom F, Barchas j, Sandler M, Usdin E, (eds) *Progress in Clinical and Biological Research*. Alan R Liss Publications, New York

Smith G (2000) Personal correspondence

Sobell MB, Sobell LC (1973) Alcoholics treated by individualized behaviour therapy: one-year treatment outcome. *Behaviour Res Therapy* **11**: 599–618

Sosnov A (2000) Personal correspondence

Sowder BJ, Burt MR (1980) *Children of heroin addicts: an assessment of health, learning, behavioural adjustment problems*. Praeger, New York: 151

Spak L, Spak F, Allebeck P (1997) Factors in childhood and youth predicting alcohol dependence and abuse in Swedish women: findings from a general population study. *Alcohol Alcohol* **32**(3): 267–74

References

Spring JA, Buss DH (1977) Three centuries of alcohol in the British diet. *Nature* **270**: 669–92

Stinson DJ, Smith WG, Amidjaya I, Kaplan JM (1979) Systems of care and treatment outcomes for alcoholic patients. *Arch Gen Psychiatry* **36**: 535–39

Strober M, Katz JL (1990) Depression in the eating disorders: a review and analysis of descriptive, family and biological findings. *Diagn Issues* **34**: 107–24

Sumption M (2001) *Retention Rates for In-Patient Reflexology Treatment of Chemical Dependence.* Awaiting publication

Sullivan JL, Stanfield CN, Maltbie AA, Hammett E, Cavener JO (1987) Stability of low blood platelet monoamine oxidase activity in human alcoholics. *Biol Psychiatry* **13**: 391–97

Thomsson H (1997) Women's smoking behaviour – caught by a cigarette diary. *Health Educ Res* **12**(2): 237–45

Turner C, Spilich GJ (1997) Research into smoking or nicotine and human cognitive performance: does the source of the funding make a difference? *Addiction* **92**(11): 1423–26

United States 84th Congress: Public Law No. 728. Narcotic Control Act, 18 July, 1956

United States Department of Health and Human Services (1990) *The Health Benefits of Smoking Cessation. A Report of the Surgeon General.* US Government Printing Office, Washington DC

Vaillant GE (1966) A 12-year follow-up of New York narcotic addicts. *Arch Gen Psychiatry* **15**: 599

Vaillant GE (1983) *The Natural History of Alcoholism: Causes, Patterns and Paths to Recovery.* Harvard University Press, Cambridge, MA

Valle SK (1981) Interpersonal functioning of alcoholism counsellors and treatment outcome. *J Study Alcohol* **42**: 783–90

Van Thiel D, Tarter R E, Rosenblaum E *et al* (1988) Ethanol, it's metabolism and gonadal effects: does sex make a difference? *Adv Alcohol Subst Abuse* **3–4**: 131–69

Veach TL, Chappel JN (1990) Physician attitudes in chemical dependency: the effects of personal experience and recovery. *Subst Abuse* **11**(2): 99

Wada K (1994) Cocaine abuse in Japan. *Japanese J Alcohol Stud Drug Dep* **29**(2): 83–91

Waddell AF, Everett ME (1980) *Drinking Behaviour Among Southwestern Indians: An Anthropological Perspective.* University of Arizona Press, Arizona

Wallace BC (1989) Psychological and environmental determinants of relapse in crack cocaine smokers. *J Subst Abuse Treat* **6**: 95–106

Wang MQ, Collins CB, DiClemente RJ, Wingwood G, Kohler CL (1998) Multiple drug use and depression: gender differences among African-Americans in high-risk community. *J Alcohol Drug Educ* **43**(1): 87–96

Weatherburn D, Lind B (1997) The impact of law enforcement activity on a heroin market. *Addiction* **92**(5): 557–69

Welsh I (1993) *Trainspotting*. Reed International Books, London

West RJ, Schneider NG (1988) Drop in heart rate following smoking cessation may be permanent. *Psychopharmacology* **94**: 566–8

White WL (1999) *Slaying the Dragon*. Chestnut Health Systems, Bloomington, Illinois

Wikler A (1948) Recent progress in research on the neurophysiological basis of morphine addiction. *Am J Psychiatry* **105**: 328–38

Wilkens W, Thiel G, Friedrich E (1997) Ecstasy: the importance of the legal status, effects and frequency of consumption. *Sucht* **43**(6): 422–9

Wills-Brandon C (1995) Public Lecture, 'Eating Disorders'. Broadway Lodge, UK

Wilsnack SC (1980) Drinking, Sexuality and Sexual Dysfunction in Women. In: Wilsnack SC, Beckman LJ (eds) *Alcohol Problems in Women*. Plenum Press, New York: 263–98

Winick C (1992) Epidemiology of Alcohol and Drug Abuse. In: Lowinson J, Ruiz P, Millman R (eds) *Substance Abuse: a comprehensive textbook*. Williams and Wilkins, Baltimore, MD

Winters KC, Weller CL, Meland JA (1993) Extent of drug abuse among juvenile offenders. *J Drug Issues* **23**(3): 515–24

Wise RA (1989) The Brain Reward. In: Liebman JM, Cooper SJ (eds) *The Neuropharmacological Basis of Reward*. Oxford University Press, Oxford

Yalom I (1991) *The Theory and Practice of Group Psychotherapy*. Basic Books, New York

Yates WR, Wilcox J, Knudson R, Myers C, Kelly MW (1990) The effect of gender and subtype on platelet MAO in alcoholism. *J Stud Alcohol* **51**: 463–7

Yesavage JA, Leirer VO, Denari M, Hollister LE (1985), Carry-over effect of marijuana intoxication on aircraft pilot performance. *Am J Psychiatry* **142**: 1325

Yu J, Perrine MWB (1997) The Transmission of parent/adult-child drinking patterns: Testing a gender-specific structural model. *Am J Drug Alc Abuse* **23**(1): 143–65

Appendix: Useful addresses

General information and advice:

National Drugs Helpline 0800 776600
National Drinkline 0800 9178282

Information on local help with drug problems across England and Wales:

Drugscope
32–36 Loman Street
London SE1 OEE
020 7928 1211
www.drugscope.org.uk

Information on local help within Scotland:

Scottish Drugs Forum
Shaftesbury House
5 Waterloo Street
Glasgow G2 6AY
0141 221 1175
www.sdf.org.uk

Information on local help in Northern Ireland:

Shaftesbury Square Hospital
116–120 Great Victoria Street
Belfast BT2 7BG
028 9032 9808

Information on local help with drink problems in UK:

Alcohol Concern
32–36 Loman Street
London SE1 OEE
020 7928 7377

Alcoholics Anonymous National Switchboard: 01904 644026
www.aa-uk.org.uk

Narcotics Anonymous National Switchboard: 020 7730 0009
www.wsoinc.com
www.ukna.org

Support for families and friends of problem drinkers:

Families Anonymous 020 7498 4680
www.famanon.org.uk

Al-Anon Families Group (UK and Eire)
(including Al-Ateen)
61 Great Dover Street
London SE1 4YF
020 7403 0888
www.hexnet.co.uk/alanon

Support for the families and friends of drug users:

ADFAM
5th floor
Epworth House
25 City Road
London EC1Y 1AA
020 7928 8900
020 7928 8898

Support for adult children of alcoholics:

ACoA England
PO Box 1576
London SW3 2XB

Scotland ACoA
c/o Andrew Melville House
65 Oakfield Avenue
Glasgow G12 8QG

www.adultchildren.org

For legal advice:

Release
388 Old Street
London EC1V 9LP
020 7603 8654
www.release.org.uk